Lost in Space-A

From Missouri to Japan and Back

Jackie Humphrey

COPYRIGHT

Jackie Humphrey
mohyfive@gmail.com
Subject line: Copyright Permission

DISCLAIMER: This work reflects the experiences of the author. The information conveyed here is for entertainment/educational purposes only. The information provided was accurate the time of the author's experience. No liability is assumed for losses or damages due to the information provided. You are responsible for your own choices, actions, and results.

DEDICATION

This book is dedicated to the men and women, young, old, and passed, who serve and have served in the Armed Forces of the United States of America. Without them, we would not be able to speak freely, write profusely, and travel unhindered. I am grateful for the many privileges that I am afforded due to their bravery.

ACKNOWLEDGEMENTS

This work could never have been accomplished without help. The Air Mobility Command has provided in-depth instruction on Space-Available travel. I am also grateful to John D's Military Space-Available (Space-A) Travel Pages (Spacea.net) as the first site I found when researching for our trip. The Space-A travelers on the Peppard.com Forum have been invaluable as well. While much of what I have learned and shared was a result of vast amounts of research, we would never have set out on this journey without the help of the many military men and women who have answered my questions via phone and email. We owe great debt also to the travelers we met who taught us numerous tricks to make our travel easier. Hopefully, we will travel again together soon.

I thank my children for teaching me to be flexible. I know that I wasn't so much when you were growing up, but, as I age, I realize that it's a great skill/quality for avoiding stress. An extra thank you goes to my Navy daughter, who pushes me to write and checks my work. I am extremely grateful to my husband, Keith, for facing the obstacles of this journey and this life with me and encouraging me to share our experience. There would be no book without you. Finally, I thank the Lord Most High for protecting us and providing for us through our fellow man.

-Jackie Humphrey

Table of Contents

INTRODUCTION

In September 2012, we started out on what we thought would be a two-week trip to see our Navy daughter in Misawa, Japan. It turns out that we had embarked on an adventure that lasted nearly four EXTRA weeks.

My husband, Keith, was a gray-area retiree, which meant that he would not get his Navy retirement benefits until his 60th birthday. We had been looking forward to a time of free travel since his actual retirement from the Navy Reserve twelve years earlier.

Keith had been stationed in Japan during his active duty years ago. Our youngest daughter was in the Navy, too. She had already been stationed in Misawa, Japan for nearly three years and was due to leave for another duty station before too long. I wanted to experience the beauty, art, and respect for humanity that they had both tried to describe to me and I wanted to go while she was still stationed there. I felt that, with her help, it would be much easier to get around and there would be folks to help guide us as we toured the area.

I wasn't wrong on that count. We met some great friends of hers who treated us as though we had always been part of the Misawa family. As a matter of fact, we met some great people all along this adventure. I'll introduce you to some of them as I take you on our journey.

I started doing research on Space-A military travel two years before our trip, investigating every web site and forum that I could find. I didn't want to go into this blind, so I armed myself with all of the information I could gather, even before applying for a passport. I learned a lot about the Space-A processes, expectations, and rules. None of that research, however, could have prepared me for the reality of Space-A travel.

I'm not going to regale you with detailed descriptions of the terminals we visited, or the restaurants we frequented, or the rooms we stayed in. You can find those all over the internet. Instead, I'm going to show you the processes that took us from A to Z. I'm going to show you the mistakes we made. I'm going to tell you about the little surprises that helped us to overcome obstacles.

I can laugh now, recounting the ups and downs, the laughter and tears. Hopefully, whether you are active duty going on leave, dependents traveling while your sponsor is deployed, or retirees like us, you'll learn things from our experiences that prevent some of the self-inflicted hardships that we faced. You may choose to do things the same way we did and figure out better solutions. Ultimately, we have to look back at this trip and smile. All in all, we had a great time and would not trade any of it…well, maybe some of it.

PREPARATION

RESEARCH AND MORE RESEARCH

There is so much to learn!

Military retirement was a big deal for Keith. It had been his goal to retire from the Navy from the day we married, so when he left active duty after twelve years because we had so many kids (four, at that time, to be exact), he was a bit disappointed that simple household economics was going to thwart his retirement dream. However, the time needed could be served in the Navy Reserve, so he enlisted for eight years of reserve duty to make his twenty years necessary for retirement.

The benefits for retirees were the same for retiring reservists as for active duty retirees with a few hitches. At the time, Reservists had to wait until their 60th birthday to collect retirement pay and receive some of the other benefits, such as medical care and free travel. That's what I was waiting for – free travel.

Fantasies of visits to exotic places have filled my brain and whet my desire for travel from the day I first learned that would be an option open to us as a couple . Later, as the family genealogist, I started listing all of the places that we could fly to, free or nearly free, to do research on our families and their history. I even started a little travel calendar in my mind, deciding which months would be the best to travel to the many U.S. military bases all over the world. This was going to be the most fulfilling time of my life. But there was a lot to learn and a lot to plan.

We're not rich folks. Keith was actually injured on his job and had back surgery shortly after his Reserve retirement and is on disability as a result of that injury. I had to rejoin the workforce after being a stay-at-home mom for years. With only an Associate degree in Liberal Arts, I wasn't trained for many lucrative professions, so money has always been a bit on the skimpy side. What we've lacked in finances, though, we've made up for in ingenuity and do-it-yourself projects.

Keith is one of those guys who can see both the negative and positive aspects of any given situation. I, on the other hand, am optimistic about anything and everything new, at least in the beginning. A year and a half before Keith's 60th birthday didn't seem too soon for research to begin.

??$$??

When our children were young, there were questions that had to be answered appropriately before they went out with friends. We wanted to know: Who will you be with? What are you going to do? Where will you be? When will you be home? How will you get there and back? Keith would have those same questions and more about this outing. How much will it cost? How much do we have? Where will we stay? Of course, most were easily answered. Keith and I would be traveling together to visit our daughter in Japan and would be home in about two weeks. How to travel was also easy to explain.

The Patriot Express is a regularly scheduled flight that goes from Seattle-Tacoma (Sea-Tac) International Airport straight to Misawa, Japan once a week. It returns to Sea-Tac the next day. It's actually a commercial flight contracted by the Department of Defense to move troops to overseas locations, so there are fees involved, but they are minute when compared to the cost of a regular commercial flight. This was going to work out perfectly.

Costs of flights were figured in, along with one or two nights lodging (just in case we were unable to catch a flight immediately). We could minimize eating expenses by shopping at commissaries or grocery stores. We've taken trips with our five children a number of times that smaller families have spent two to five times the money that we did. We learned to cut costs, finding things to do that weren't expensive but just as much fun. Making memories doesn't have to mean spending money that you don't have. I know quite a few retirees, both military and civilian, who have made the same decision about their own lifestyles.

Answering Keith's questions meant that I would have to research, plan, present, then research, plan, and present again until he was satisfied that a trip halfway around the world was feasible and affordable. That's why I went to work on the research so far in advance. Japan was chosen because, and while, our daughter was there.

In the meantime, she went on temporary assignment out of Japan. She would not be back there when we first became eligible for travel, but would return about seven months later. That gave us a little more time to plan.

She called us one day from Afghanistan. "So, daughter," I broached, "we were thinking that, since you won't be able to come home on your way back from Afghanistan, we would come to see you in Misawa."

"Wow, Mom, would you? That would be awesome! I have two bedrooms so you can stay with me and I'll pay for everything while you're there. You just have to get there. That would be great!" She seemed pretty excited at the prospect.

Keith already had his passport, so I had still had to get mine. I was also putting away a little bit of money each week. Staying with our daughter in Misawa meant we wouldn't have lodging expenses. That would make this trip easy to fund.

PHONE MARATHON

On September 14, I called Sea-Tac Air Mobility Command Desk to verify how many seats were available on this week's flight. I was told that there were tentatively 45 seats available for that Sunday's flight. The only problem would be getting to Sea-Tac.

We live in central Missouri, in the woods. We're a quarter of a mile from our nearest neighbor, a mile from the blacktop, and fifteen miles from the nearest town, where the population is only twenty-seven hundred.

The nearest base, Scott Air Force Base, is about three hours away. Scott has flights in and out almost daily, but on the particular weekend that we were ready to leave on our journey, Scott was having an Air Show – no flights out that weekend. I was back and forth from my computer room/guest bedroom to the living room trying to figure out the when, where and how of starting this trip. Having scoured the Facebook pages of a number of military passenger terminals, I was finally armed with a plan.

I told Keith that Scott AFB didn't have any flights going to the West Coast until the next week. It was the afternoon of September 13th. As we sat in our living room, we agreed that we wanted to leave as soon as possible so we could be home by October 1. "I'm willing to drive eight hours to get to a base that will get us to Sea-Tac for the Patriot Express," he stated. "That will be a piece of cake considering how far we are going."

"Done," I replied, heading back to the office. "I know there's a flight from Wright-Patterson Air Force Base in Ohio to Naval Air Station Whidbey Island on Saturday. I just have to make sure we can get from Whidbey to Sea-Tac by Sunday morning."

I scoured the net and found that Whidbey Island has a free bus from NAS to an island ferry to Seattle, which was also free. From the ferry to Sea-Tac on city buses would take a couple of hours, but the busses ran until late in the evening. The cost was less than ten dollars each. A quick call to the terminal at NAS Whidbey Island gave me the arrival time of the flight we intended to catch from Wright-Pat. We would arrive in plenty of time to get to Sea-Tac by 10 p.m. on Saturday. The USO at Sea-Tac is open 24/7 and we would be able to rest there until roll call on Sunday morning.

It was time to pack.

GOING TO JAPAN

WE'RE OFF!

While the Patriot Express allows seventy-pound bags to be checked on their flights, I knew that we might not be able to get on certain flights on our return trip with such a large load. We made a conscious decision to make sure that our bags would be allowed on ANY aircraft that was going our way. This meant that each only carried a couple of changes of clothes, an extra pair of shoes, extra underwear and socks, a jacket, knit hat, and NO laptop. By the way…jackets are REALLY important. It can get super cold up in the clouds on those large planes with little or no heat!

It seemed as though we were only packing for a nearby overnighter, but when we weighed our bags at home, we knew that they would be a good fit for even the smallest craft. Keith's bag weighed eighteen pounds; mine only weighed eleven pounds. We had plenty of weight left over to carry food so that we wouldn't have to spend a lot in restaurants.

I didn't sleep well that night because I was so excited about seeing our daughter. I was excited about traveling in general. It was a well-discussed subject for several years and now it was finally going to happen. I couldn't wait.

Friday morning was spent verifying that all of the flight information I had was still current. We did not want to waste an eight hour drive. Since I hadn't written down any of my questions, I ended up calling the Wright-Patterson terminal about six times that morning. I was pretty sure that the young lady who was answering my questions was getting quite tired of my voice.

The only thing yet unplanned was our departure from home. If we left on Friday afternoon, we would have to find somewhere to sleep. The terminal at Wright-Pat is normally closed on Saturday. However, if there is a flight scheduled, it opens about two hours before departure. Consequently, we knew that the terminal would not open until about 10:30 or 11 a.m. We would have had to leave home around midnight. We decided to leave on Friday so we would have a minimum of night driving. But where would we sleep, other than in the car?

On one more call to the USO at Dayton International Airport, I spoke with a wonderful gentleman who told me that the USO was unmanned after 11 p.m. He did say, however, that the gate into the area was never locked and that there was a sofa and two recliners that we would be welcome to use overnight and that the office would reopen at 8 a.m.

That settled that.

FRIDAY, SEPTEMBER 14

About noon, we loaded up the car, turned off the water and all non-essential electric, said goodbye to our cats, and locked up our home. Keith's best friend had agreed to come by every two or three days to feed our outside cats and make sure the place hadn't burned down.

I had printed maps and schedules of every bus, ferry or train that we needed to get from Whidbey Island, northwest of Seattle, to Sea-Tac. I also had the same for the route from Joint Base Lewis-McChord, which is southwest of Seattle, as I had originally thought we would be able to find a flight from Scott AFB to McChord. We had about $500 in traveling money and we were going to Japan.

The drive to Ohio was pretty uneventful. We made a few stops in town to pick up snacks and gas up, leaving Missouri around 4 p.m. Keith drove the entire distance. We stopped to rest along the way, arriving at Dayton International about midnight. Finding our way to the USO, we verified with a guard that we could go into the area. Keith chose a recliner and I promptly stretched out on the sofa. By 1 a.m., we were both sound asleep.

Saturday, September 15

After about an hour, we were both awakened by loud noises coming from the gate next to the counter. A lady in a wheelchair was coming in to rest, too. By the time she settled into the other recliner, it was nearly 3 a.m. We didn't have to been at Wright-Pat until much later in the morning, but the lights in the terminal, along with the regular TSA announcements, kept us both from getting much more rest. Back to the car and heading to Wright-Pat, about five miles away, at 6 a.m. seemed the prudent thing to do. We could nap in the car if necessary.

WRIGHT-PATTERSON AIR FORCE BASE, OHIO

We didn't nap. Grabbing breakfast at McDonald's, we set out to find the gate into Wright-Patterson. There was a marathon on the base that day, causing many streets to be roped off. Combine that with one-way streets and the GPS on my phone was fairly worthless. We found Wal-Mart while searching for a way into the base, so we stopped and bought a couple of neck pillows for sleeping on the flights. They became a very important part of our luggage. We also bought a small gift for the young lady at Wright-Pat who had answered so many of my phone calls the day before. We reached at the terminal at 8:30 a.m., plenty of time to spare.

The air around Wright-Pat's terminal was crisp. The marathon route ran right past the front of the terminal, so we were privileged to see all of the runners as they ran the course. A band from a local church was playing music and shouting encouragement to the runners, many of whom responded with thumbs up or a wave. Children of band members stood on the sidewalk, clapping and waving, yelling "Good job!" and "You can do it!" to the marathoners. It was clear that all involved were having a great time, making it easy to join in.

Around 9:30 a.m., we noticed a car parking near the terminal. Three men got out and checked the door. Finding that it was locked, two of them went back to their car. Keith decided that they were probably going to catch the same flight we were going on.

We walked over to the building, saw the man was wearing a Navy ball cap, and Keith immediately offered his hand to the man. "I just noticed your cap," he said, breaking the ice. "You're going Space-A, too?"

The man acknowledged that he was. Within minutes, they were talking as though they had been friends for eons. It's that way when you're a veteran, you know, especially when you've been in the same branch of service. Camaraderie springs up quickly. The other two men joined us as we waited at the door. We talked and laughed there for nearly an hour on that sunny but cool September morning. Within a few hours, we would all five be westward bound, all for different final destinations. One was going home to San Diego, one to the area around Travis Air Force Base. The third hadn't quite decided on his final destination yet. He was just leaving his Missouri home to travel for a few weeks before winter hit.

When the terminal was finally opened that morning, we were welcomed by Bob. My telephone friend didn't work on Saturday, so I left her gift with Bob. He then verified our sign up status, weighed and checked our bags, laughing and joking all the while. It was a very pleasant experience in a small terminal. Once we were all checked in, we waited for the crew to let Bob know that they were ready for us to board and he promptly took us to a waiting van and drove us out to the tarmac.

The plane we boarded was a commercial type aircraft with front facing seats. Many that we flew in after that original flight were C-130 or similar planes that had side facing seats. Since there were only five of us, we had our choice of where to sit. The crew was very congenial and we were off to a great start.

The flight was peaceful. Keith and I both napped for a couple of hours during the flight. We were well rested when we arrived at the passenger terminal at NAS Whidbey Island about five hours later.

NAS WHIDBEY ISLAND, WASHINGTON

The terminal was empty save for the five of us that just arrived and two sailors manning the counter.

I immediately called Sea-Tac to verify seat status on the Patriot Express for the next morning. Much to my dismay, tentative seats had dropped to 35 and the flight was rescheduled until Monday morning due to a typhoon off the coast of Japan. We had an extra day to wait.

No problem! I called the Visitor's Quarters on base, found a room for $40 and made a reservation. We could spend the night at NAS Whidbey and make the trek to Sea-Tac the next morning. One of the sailors on duty offered to drive us to the room as it was about a mile to walk. We graciously accepted. He not only took us to check in, but also took us on a quick tour of the base. It had been a long time since I had seen the ocean and I was ecstatic to be there.

After unpacking our bags, Keith and I grabbed a quick snack at a base restaurant and then walked a couple of miles along the base jogging trail that follows the shoreline. The sound of the waves crashing against the jutting rocks near the base campground is still etched in my mind. The campground has several small buildings called yurts for rent, but they were all occupied. Had we packed a tent, I knew where I really wanted to sleep. But we had a day of carrying gym bags scheduled on the morrow, so a good night's sleep in a bed seemed most sane.

SUNDAY, SEPTEMBER 16

We slept well, up and ready to go at about 8 a.m. I had washed and dried our laundry before Keith got up, so I was antsy to get started on our trek. I pulled out the bus and ferry schedules, checking to see how soon the next bus would be leaving the main gate. My jaw dropped.

The bus did not run on Sunday! How, oh, how had I missed that? All of my careful planning suddenly seemed for naught. I called the front desk and asked if there was a shuttle to Sea-Tac or at least to the ferry. "No, ma'am, but there is a taxi," replied the distant voice on the phone. I breathed a little easier as she gave me the number.

"Forty dollars," the man said, "to the ferry."

Ouch, I thought. This could be bad.

Out loud, I told myself, "Okay! Breathe! Relax! We can figure this out." Keith just watched and waited. "We may have to hitchhike," I told him, "just down to the ferry. If we can get a ride from someone on base to the ferry, we'll be okay. The city buses in Seattle do run on Sunday."

He groaned. "Hitchhiking isn't legal on base."

"Then we can wait until we get out of the main gate. We don't have a whole lot of options here." Tears were welling up as I apologized for this awful mistake. "I'm very sorry. I should have checked the schedule before we got the room."

He pulled me close and held me while I cried. "It's okay," he said. "We'll figure out something."

I dried my tears; we picked up our bags, and headed out into the sunshine. I prayed silently as we turned toward the office in the building across the street. "God, please get us to Seattle, quickly and safely."

As we hiked toward the office, I stopped a couple of drivers leaving the parking lot, asking if they were going anywhere near

Seattle or the ferry. None were. I queried the lady at the desk, hoping that she knew someone who would be willing to take us for a fee. She again suggested the taxi.

Out the door we went, toward the main gate. No hitchhiking on base, Keith had said, so we made our way the rest of the way to the gate without stopping any more drivers. As we got closer to the base exit, a young sailor on foot caught up with us at the turnstile. Keith stepped aside to let him by, but the young man stepped back and waved us through.

"We're quite a bit slower moving than you are," Keith smiled as he spoke to the young gentleman.

"That's okay. I'm not in a big hurry. I'm just walking home," he said. Straight ahead of us, about a block away were townhouses that very much resembled a home that Keith and I had lived in when we were first married, living in Navy housing.

"So you live right there?" I ventured. He nodded so I continued. "Do you know anyone who might be willing to take us to the ferry for gas money? We were going to take the bus, but didn't realize that the bus doesn't run on Sunday."

He only paused a second. "I have a couple of friends at my house that work at Everett (Naval Station). They might be able to take you. I just live right over here. Let's go see." We followed him another fifty yards and he turned toward a building. "This is mine."

He led us in the front door. The unfurnished living room with its plain white walls definitely felt military. He quickly went upstairs while we lowered our bags to the floor. We waited.

About five minutes later, he came back down the stairs with another young man quickly following. The second sailor introduced himself.

"Hi, I'm T. J. I understand that you need a ride to Sea-Tac." Keith and I said yes in unison as we nodded. "I'll be glad to give you a ride. It may take a little while to get my buddy upstairs moving, though. He's not feeling so hot."

We didn't care how long it took. We expressed our deep appreciation, knowing that this ride would save us a lot of grief.

It was a little bit chilly that morning, so I sat on the living room floor leaning against the wall while Keith, T. J., and Nicolas, as we found out was the first man's name, stood on the rear patio, smoking and talking about their Navy. After about ten minutes, when I realized they weren't coming back in after their cigarettes, I went to the patio door. "Let me take your pictures, boys. I'll need this for my trip diary when I explain to people how you saved us." They laughed and smiled and joked about mug shots, moving as I directed them.

T. J. was from Utah and Nicolas hailed from South Africa via Texas. We heard stories from them about their homes, their families, and their plans for the future. We chatted until about an hour later, when their cohort came up to the patio door, groaning, wrapped up in a blanket. "Too much partying last night?" Keith grinned. "Been there, done that."

"Actually, no, I've been feeling bad since Thursday and came up here anyway, thinking I would get better." He told us that he had been running a fever and coughing for several days and now just wanted to sleep.

"Well, you can sleep in the truck," T. J. told him. "These folks need some breakfast so we need to get on the road." We said goodbye to Nicolas and thanked him for listening to us out on the road and not passing us by. Keith tied our bags down in the fully loaded bed of T.J.'s extended cab Dodge truck and we climbed into the rear seat.

Matt, T.J.'s sick friend, lived at Whidbey Island when his own father was in the Navy. His parents still live very near Seattle, so he was pretty excited to get a duty station so close to his family. He directed T. J. to Wal-Mart so he could get medicine.

The three of us went into the store while Keith waited outside, guarding the open truck bed. After we picked out the generic cold capsules for Matt, I stopped at the Subway counter to get lunch for Keith and me. Once we all had food and drink, we were on our way again.

Matt directed T.J. over Deception Pass on Skagit Bay at the north end of Puget Sound. I'm especially fond of the ocean, so I was taking pictures like crazy. The views in the area are beautiful, and as we rode through, I told Keith that this is, indeed, a place we should visit when we are not on a time schedule. He agreed.

The drive to the Navy base at Everett, which is about forty-five miles north of Sea-Tac, should have taken about thirty minutes or so, but T. J., a gracious host, took us on a little tour of the area, explaining that he usually spent his Sundays driving, taking in the sights. So, the ride was a bit longer than we anticipated, but we were able to experience some of the beauty of the state of Washington.

SEA-TAC, SEATTLE, WASHINGTON

I'd like to make a little plug here for the USO. Most USO locations are very adept at making service members and their families feel welcome and appreciated. Some facilities are better equipped than others, with everything from eating areas and internet cafes to sleeping areas. Some have only a television area. Some are better manned than others and open 24/7 to serve our military. Some are so desperate for volunteers that they operate unmanned rooms to sit in, with books, magazines and games available.

The USO at Sea-Tac is especially amazing. When we passed through on this trip, they were located on the 2nd floor of the airport. If they ran out of room to store luggage, they had a separate storage room, although it was a good little walk to get there. There was a television room with about twenty-five recliners to enjoy the big screen TV. Six or eight internet café stations lined the wall of the main room, with several sofas and recliners to seat another ten to fifteen people. The kitchen area sported a counter with stools on one wall and several tables to enjoy food and drink. The quiet sleeping room had bunks for twelve and there was also a shower to freshen up before or after your nap. The volunteers that we came in contact with were all attentive, kind, and understanding of needs. I was quite impressed.

Sea-Tac is a civilian airport but the procedures for getting on the Patriot Express are nearly the same as in a military facility. We had plenty of time before the 5:30 a.m. roll call for the flight to Misawa on Monday morning, but by the time we checked in as present to the AMC office, there were only twenty-four tentative seats. Looking around the USO, we couldn't tell who was trying to get on the PE and who was flying to somewhere else on the mainland. There was nothing to do but wait.

Keith watched football on TV. I read a book. We napped. We ate. We went for walks around the airport. We watched people. We talked to people.

As I watched service people and their families come in and out of the USO that night, one young lady caught my attention. She was traveling with her two children, a girl about three years old and a boy who was probably nearing age two. I sat at the table next to theirs during a meal and overheard her talking to those young ones.

She sounded like me, over thirty years ago. I listened as she answered questions matter-of-factly and gave directions in tones that, while spoken with love, required adherence. Her son, finished with his food, came and stood right next to me, watching me stir my tea. I smiled at him. He smiled back.

Monday, September 17

One of the Space-A rules is that if you are selected for a flight, you must have all of your bags, both for check in and carry on, with you, ready to be weighed and tagged immediately. As the time for roll call closed in, folks started getting their bags and heading down to the first floor of the terminal, not wanting to be late.

I saw the young mother, Jenell, whose husband was in the Air Force, struggling to get out of the door with two large bags, a stroller and her children. I offered to help her get down to the waiting area by the ticket counter and then would come back to help Keith get our own bags. He was fast asleep in the TV lounge and I didn't want to wake him until the last possible moment anyway.

She was quite grateful to have help. I held the little girl's hand and pulled a wheeled suitcase behind me. Mom pushed the little guy in the stroller and pulled the other suitcase.

Jenell and I talked along the way. Although the walk was only about five minutes long, we learned quite a bit about one another, I realized that we had a few things in common. At thirty, she was the mother of two, first a girl, Zayla, born one month before her 27th birthday, then a boy, Lennon, nineteen months later. How uncanny! My own oldest, also a girl, was born about a month before my 27th birthday! My son was born eighteen months later. Both of our names start with J and both of our husbands' names start with K. Her husband would transfer next year as is our daughter. We both met and dated our husbands nearly two years before we were married. We were both raised in the Catholic Church. We were both on our way to Misawa, Japan. We think alike on many levels. By the time we reached the 1st level of the terminal, we were fast friends.

When Keith and I came down with our own bags, we sat next to the small family and I introduced him to Jenell. She was traveling without her husband and was in Category 5. When we looked around at how many young military people were waiting in the area, mostly service members on leave, we knew her prospects for getting on the flight to Misawa could be pretty slim and that ours were virtually nil. Other retirees were waiting, too, and you could tell that some of the more experienced travelers already knew the score.

We waited for the announcements. Sure enough, the highest category chosen was only Category III for the twenty-eight available seats. There was no chance that we were going to Misawa today. However, because the Misawa flight was a day late, there was another flight to Yokota, Japan the next morning. Nearly five hundred miles from Misawa, at least it was in Japan. Hopefully, because the plane was full today, there would be less people trying to make Yokota's flight. We would wait for tomorrow's opportunity.

Keith and I helped Jenell get her bags and children back up to the USO. She sat them down at a table in the kitchen area and brought them toast and juice. Keith and I sat at the table next to theirs with hot drinks. We all talked about how to handle the delay.

Jenell and her children had already spent at least one night at a nearby hotel and she was determined not to spend money again. She decided that she would stay at the USO until the next morning's roll call. We didn't even consider a hotel room as an option. The bunks at the USO would be sufficient for us, so that was our decision, too.

I was sipping a cup of hot tea when Lennon, got down from his chair and gave me a big grin. He reached for his sippy cup from his table, and then stood there, sipping, grinning, sipping, and grinning. When Zayla saw the attention he was getting, she climbed down from her chair and stood next to him, giggling. Then she made a move I didn't expect. She sidled up to me and put her little hand in mine.

I shrugged my shoulders at Jenell. "I guess they can tell I'm a granny," I offered with a smile.

She grinned back. "I think so," she replied. "They left their grandparents in North Carolina a few days ago and I think they miss them already."

By 9 a.m., few of us were left in the USO. We notice several retired couples, but they didn't stay long. I read for a while, helped take the kiddos for a walk around the terminal, and took a nap soon after lunch.

After napping for several hours, Keith and I went for a walk out to the smoking area. It was such a nice day, only a couple more hours of sunshine were left. I was beginning to feel cooped up. I kept thinking about how those children must be feeling, too, in the family room that may seem big when you only have to be there for an hour, but shrinks in size as the stay grows longer. I asked Keith if we could help bring them outside for a little while. Although he wasn't tickled pink with the idea, he did agree that they probably could use some air. We headed back upstairs to get them.

Jenell was again very grateful for the help. She loaded necessary jackets and water cups onto the stroller and off we went, up and down the sidewalk in front of the baggage area of the terminal. By the time we got back to the smoking area at the end of the terminal, we had decided to venture away to locate another food source than the USO. Jenell mentioned that she saw several restaurants near the hotel they had stayed in, and that it was just a short walk. We headed down the street one block and were out of the airport property. A right turn showed us several eating establishments only a few blocks away.

At 4:30 on a Monday afternoon in Seattle, the streets are loaded with traffic. I held Zayla's hand firmly as we took in the sights along the way. Children can open your eyes to so many wonders that we certainly take for granted. Pigeons scavenging on the sidewalk excited them. A small waterfall in the courtyard of a hotel mesmerized them. They giggled as they saw themselves in the mirrored window of a beauty salon. A sprinkler system became a gauntlet to race through. The walk to Jack-in-the-Box was short, but fascinating for them.

<u>Tuesday, September 18</u>

Tuesday morning found us all waiting together again, hoping that this time, we will be on our way. There were sixty-six seats available for this flight. Finally, Jenell and her children were chosen and they were going home. But as name after name was called we felt our hope swirling, swirling down the drain. We were not going to Japan today either.

I hugged Jenell and her children as they were leaving to board the Yokota flight on Tuesday morning. We were close enough by now that we cried as we said our goodbyes and parted.

Keith and I trudged back to the USO as did one of the other retiree couples that we had seen the day before. We were sitting at tables next to each other while Keith and I discussed our options. I had noticed this lady yesterday. She was tall and slender, a slight reddish cast to her hair, twinkling eyes and a mischievous smile. She was soft-spoken and when she talked with her husband, I heard just a touch of a southern drawl. Her husband was a little stocky, receding hair line and a short salt and peppered mustache. I had seen his smile, too, almost as mischievous as hers. The both seemed a little disheartened at the moment, just like we were.

Okay, now what? There are three flights to Japan each week from Sea-Tac: Sunday's flight to Misawa, Tuesday's flight to Yokota and Thursday's flight to Kadena. A quick check of the Sea-Tac Facebook page told me that there was only one seat available on Thursday and only nineteen to Misawa on Sunday. Our experience thus far made us believe that there was no way we were going to get on the Sunday flight. But what were the options? I suggested that we might take a bus to Joint Base Lewis-McChord, and try to find flights to southern California with the potential of going to the long way around to get to Japan. This meant that we would be going through Hawaii to get to Japan.

Maggie overheard us. She introduced herself and her husband, Johnny, and asked if I knew how to get to McChord AFB because they were thinking about doing the same thing. I offered that they could just follow us to the bus.

It didn't take long for Maggie's true self to appear. This lady who had seemed so quiet and docile in the terminal had a sharp wit, and found Keith to be a convenient target. He had made some fairly innocuous comments when we met Maggie and Johnny that displayed his prowess at sarcasm and wit. As we waited for the bus outside the terminal, Maggie saw an opportunity for a friendly jab. I don't remember what her comment was. I just remember that it stunned us and I laughed so hard that I almost cried. The bus ride was hilarious as they parried back and forth, leaving only a minute or two for breathing room between pokes.

JOINT BASE LEWIS-MCCHORD, WASHINGTON

Through two bus rides and the mile and a half walk through the gate to the Evergreen Inn at McChord, we enjoyed the camaraderie of these similar travelers. We traded stories about our homes, kids, retirement, health…you name it. We had great conversations.

Maggie and Johnny had wheels on their small suitcases while Keith and I carried gym bags. Maggie and I walked a little ahead of Johnny and Keith, checking our maps, getting our bearings. We were about a half a mile from the inn when Maggie spied a sign.

"Jackie," she put her hand out and stopped me. "Look, there's a thrift store over there."

I chuckled. "I don't need to buy more stuff to carry, Maggie!"

"No, no! They might have a suitcase with wheels over there! Then you guys wouldn't have to carry your bags." She was definitely concerned about Keith's back. In sharing earlier, I had told her about the accident that Keith had at work years before and the subsequent surgery and disability.

Keith and Johnny seemed okay with taking a respite from the walking. We left the bags with them and Maggie and I trekked over to the base thrift shop about two hundred yards away.

What a delight that it was actually open! Many base thrift stores are only open a few hours a week because they are operated mostly on volunteer hours. This store was huge and I counted about fifteen volunteers and employees. A large sign near a far corner from the entrance pointed us to the luggage shelves.

There must have been fifty bags of all different types on the two stacks of shelves and the floor in front of them. We both started grabbing potential purchases, checking for wheels and zippers and work. I finally settled on a scrapbook case with wheels and handle. The price was $20, a small price to pay to save backs.

While I stood in line, Maggie went to check the clearance area to see if there were any other bags that might be better and/or cheaper. A woman after my own heart, she came back with one that was only $8, but upon further investigation, we found that the zipper didn't work.

I paid for my purchase and we headed back to our men. We'd only been gone from them for about twenty minutes, but they both wisecracked about us being there all day. They quickly quieted, however, when they saw that the contents of one gym bag and our food bag all fit perfectly in the wheeled suitcase. We continued on our way to the Inn, pretty happy with the outcome of that little side trip. Hunger moved us along, in a hurry to get settled in our rooms and find dinner.

There was a refrigerator of cold drinks for sale in the lobby of the Evergreen Inn. Johnny bought a round for all of us, beer for him and Maggie and Keith, wine for me. After dropping our bags in our rooms, we all met at the pavilion behind the inn and enjoyed time off our feet. We discussed getting signed in at the passenger terminal and then we would have dinner together. Maggie offered to line up the taxi to the terminal.

First, though, a nap.

I woke up before any of the others. Feeling energetic and refreshed, I called Maggie and asked her to hang on about getting a taxi. Then I went out to find a ride for us. About ten servicemen were hanging out at the pavilion where we had earlier shared drinks with Maggie and Johnny.

I didn't feel the least bit of trepidation as I walked up to the group. "Anybody here have a car?"

A young man raised his arm. "I do, ma'am. How can I help you?" Oh, how I love the military!

Consider too, that I'm calling a thirty-five year old guy young. At my age, it is. "I have a couple of retired guys that don't want to walk any more today," I told him. "We need a ride to the passenger terminal to sign in for a Space-A flight, if you can help us out."

"Be glad to, ma'am. My car is parked right over there," as he pointed to the parking lot about two hundred feet away, "and I can take you whenever you're ready."

"Thank you very much! I'll get them together and be right back."

There was a little bit of extra bounce in my step as I went to get Maggie, Johnny, and Keith. The Master Sergeant not only waited for us at the passenger terminal while we signed in, but he then took us to the BX on base so we could get dinner.

We ate a good meal. After dinner, Maggie remembered a couple of things she needed to pick up. On the walk back to our rooms, we talked about our homes, and she encouraged us to consider Charleston if we ever decided to leave Missouri.

After our return, it took about an hour and a half to complete our load of laundry. By then, Keith and I were both ready for a good night's sleep.

WEDNESDAY, SEPTEMBER 19

I must say that I loved the Evergreen Inn. I didn't love it because the rooms were magnificent. I loved it because of the sergeant at the front desk.

This young woman represented the utmost in customer service. On the survey at the end of our stay I gave her tens on a five-point scale. Everything about her appearance was squared away. Her winning smile and politeness, paying attention to the smallest clues about our needs, won my heart. How long would we be staying? We didn't know. Check-in was a breeze with her and she thoroughly understood our situation in traveling Space-A. She offered maps of the base, directions to everywhere we wanted to go. She was apologetic that there was no base shuttle but there was a taxi.

I was up early as usual on Wednesday morning, checking Facebook pages, calling terminals, figuring out our next move. Good news! There was a flight that afternoon to Travis Air Force Base and from Travis we could easily get to Hawaii. I called Maggie. The four of us met for our continental breakfast and discussed the new schedule. Roll call for the flight to Travis was later that morning. It was time to pack.

Since checkout was at 11 a.m., we knew we had to give up our rooms. However, when we gathered at the front desk and spoke with the sergeant, she suggested that she could make new, unconfirmed reservations for us. If we were not chosen for the flight, we would have reservations; if we did leave on the flight, the reservations would fall off the books at 6 p.m. While I was taking her picture, I asked her how long it would take the taxi to get there and if she knew how much it would cost to get us to the terminal.

"I'll take you," she said. "I get a fifteen minute break and I'll use it to take you to the terminal."

I looked at her in unbelief and she just grinned back at me. "Won't you get in trouble? I don't want you to get in any trouble at all. I just gave you a great survey!"

She shook her head. "No, it's my break and I can use it however I like. I'll just tell them you're my aunt."

"Why?" I was still unbelieving.

"Because I like you guys," she explained. "You're fun and you're nice. We don't get a lot of fun people up here at the desk. We do get a lot of nasty complaints. I'll be outside in a few minutes."

She finished making our reservations and announced to her coworkers that she was going on break.

True to her word, she met us outside the main entrance and led us to her truck. We threw our bags in the bed and the four of us climbed in to the extended cab. She shared that she was soon to be transferred to Korea. She also told us that if the flight was cancelled or if we didn't get selected to call the front desk and she would come back to the airfield to take us back to the Evergreen Inn. The drive to the terminal only lasted a few minutes, but that girl made an impression on me that I won't soon forget.

Once at the terminal, we verified that there was still a flight scheduled for today and that our sign in from the previous day was still valid. There were plenty of seats on this flight and the terminal was empty save for three other people. Roll call went quickly and we began the two hour wait for departure. The USO is located in the terminal, so the four of us found a table, got sandwiches and drinks. The two computers were in use by volunteers, but we really had no need of them at the moment. We had a flight to catch today. Tomorrow the schedule will probably change anyway.

The Air Force staff at the McChord terminal was quite helpful, too. No matter how many times one of us went to the counter, we were greeted with smiles and helpful attitudes. They seemed as excited as we were as they checked our bags and processed through to the departure gate. Boarding time arrived, and, as a young airman approached us, we gathered up our jackets and prepared to leave the waiting area.

"I'm very sorry," he began. "The plane that you were scheduled on is a Med-Evac. Unfortunately, it's broken and will not be going out today."

"What are the chances that it will be fixed quickly and still be going later?" Maggie queried.

The airman shook his head. "I'm so sorry, ma'am. It's what we call 'hard' broke. It will take at least twelve hours to fix and it may not even go then." He informed us that there were no other flights going anywhere that day, but there was one scheduled for Thursday morning.

I called the Evergreen Inn. "May I speak with the sergeant, please?"

"May I tell her who's calling, ma'am?"

"Yes, please, it's her aunt."

I got off the phone and told the grinning threesome that she would be there in twenty minutes to pick us up.

Getting back into rooms was a piece of cake with my 'niece' working. She had us quickly settled, although in other rooms than we'd had the night before. No problem.

Johnny stopped by the bulletin board as we were going to our rooms. "Hey, look here," he said, pointing at a flyer. "Dinner and bingo at the club at 5 o'clock. I say we make it a date." It was already 3 p.m.

"Sounds good to me," Keith answered. "I'm not any good at bingo but I like to eat."

Maggie chuckled as we agreed to meet in the lobby in fifteen minutes. The walk is only about a half mile and the weather was beautiful, although smoke from fires in other parts of Washington blocked what should have been a beautiful view of Mount Rainier.

The club was fairly empty when we got there. The only place open for business at the time was a dark little bar at the back of the building. We sat at a round wooden table next to a wall, perfect for watching people come and go. Beer for the threesome, water for me, we munched on too much popcorn before a meal.

Leaving the bar a few minutes before 5 p.m., we were all salivating as we walked toward the smells of chicken and roast beef. This dinner was free for club members. Johnny and Maggie were members and brought us as guests. We thoroughly enjoyed this home style meal after all of the sandwiches we'd been consuming for the past week.

Bingo was also free, but you could buy extra cards for fifty cents each. There were only two games, so this was not destined to be a night on the town. Rather, it was a break from what seemed to be hectic travel. None of us won anything, but we had a good time working at it.

The walk back to our rooms was quick but peaceful. It was just dusk and the evening air was a starting to chill a little, and Maggie started feeling like she had a cold coming on. We hurried back to the rooms to get her out of the brisk air.

Before bed that night, I called the terminal to see if there was any change on the flight to Travis. Yes, it had been cancelled completely, but there was another flight to Travis with roll call at 8 p.m. Thursday evening.

I rang Maggie and told her about the change, letting her know that we didn't have to go to the terminal early in the morning. We set a time to meet for breakfast in the morning and said goodnight.

THURSDAY, SEPTEMBER 20

Thursday morning was a bit gloomy. The sky was overcast. There were even a few drops of rain as we left for the breakfast room that morning. Maggie and Johnny were already there when Keith and I arrived. After we greeted each other and set about consuming bagels and fruit, Maggie made an announcement.

"We're going to call it quits and go home." Keith and I, dumbfounded, stopped all movement and stared at her as she spoke. "Johnny has a doctor's appointment in a couple of weeks and we don't want to take a chance that he'll miss that, so we're going home and try to do this another time." I knew that wasn't all. "Plus I'm not feeling so good and I really need to get some rest."

We protested, but not too much. I felt bad that Maggie felt bad. Keith and I had found new comrades in Johnny and Maggie. We enjoyed the time that we spent with them very much. We had already talked about how hard it was going to be, separating from them, when we split off to go to Japan while they went to Korea. Now it was going to be even sooner. Our disappointment was impossible to hide.

The rest of our breakfast time together was spent discussing their possibilities for getting home quickly. There was a flight to the East Coast on Saturday and they planned on picking that up. Meanwhile, they would extend their stay at Evergreen Inn one more day. They also reiterated an earlier invitation to visit them in

Charleston and hoped that we would just hang out with them until we had to be at the terminal.

We all went to the front desk together again that morning. Keith and I checked out while Johnny tried to extend his room one more day. But our sergeant apologized that he could not keep his room due to reservists coming to the base for duty that weekend. All rooms were booked. However, they did have rooms available in another building, in a different area of the base. Johnny was glad to take it, but it was too far to walk with baggage. Once again, my little 'niece' volunteered to transport us. We dropped all of our bags at their new digs and walked to the club for lunch.

The hazy day started to clear up as we were passing the base medical clinic. Maggie, feeling much worse today, decided to see a doctor for a prescription to keep the effects of this cold to a minimum, so we passed the afternoon waiting for her to be squeezed in between scheduled appointments at the base medical center. It was nearly 4:30 p.m. when we left the building and made our way back to their room for our bags.

I didn't cry when we left them. We had laughed so much together. I would greatly miss their humor. Johnny insisted that if there was any problem with our flight we must come back and stay with them. After hugs and pictures, we told them we would and wished them a safe journey home.

We left them standing on the sidewalk, waving to us as we crossed the street, moving on the next chapter.

As we passed the parking area of a nearby basketball court, twenty men finished a game and started walking to their cars. An opportunity! I asked if any of them would be driving near the passenger terminal. Several said yes, while one, little louder than the others, added "Sure, I'll take you there." It moved our focus quickly from the loss of Maggie and Johnny's company to the venture at hand. We were back at the terminal in ten minutes.

Food at the USO was the highest priority when we arrived since we had a few hours before roll call. We settled in with our bags.

Roll call again went pretty smoothly. We repeated check-in, and this time we were actually on the plane! We were starting the next leg of this trip, finally, after five days in Washington.

No, we weren't!

On the runway for over thirty minutes, it was finally announced that the flight controls were not working properly. Although I was glad that safety was the number one priority, I was sad that we were not going anywhere once again. It was nearly midnight, and although we had promised that we would call Johnny and Maggie if there was a problem with our flight, Maggie wasn't feeling well and we were not going to wake them.

Staff advised us that there was a flight to the Marine Corps Base at Miramar, California in the morning. Flying into Miramar opened several more doors for us. There are two bases to fly from in the area. Naval Air Station North Island, California is only twenty miles away, which can easily be traversed by bus.

Our immediate problem was where to go while we waited. The terminal was only open at this hour because of the flight that had been scheduled to depart. Once luggage was returned to the passengers, we were all expected to leave the terminal, but most of us had checked out of our rooms and there were no vacancies on base. The nearest Denny's was a $20 cab ride away. While the staff did their best to delay closing as long as possible, Keith and I were still without a solution when they finally locked the doors at 1:30 a.m. They would reopen at 5 a.m. Friday.

It was about fifty-five degrees that night, colder than we really liked. We found a little alcove at the end of the terminal, a double-door entrance to an area that was out of operation. We set up camp.

We sat on our neck pillows, insulating our bottoms from the cold concrete. Our bags, stacked sideways on a cart, served as a much-needed windbreak. We were wearing medium-weight jackets and we had ball caps and stocking caps to shield the light from our eyes and keep our ears warm. It took a little while to get comfortable enough to nap, but we finally did.

<u>Friday, September 21</u>

I didn't nap for long. I was awake, waiting for the doors to open, at 4 a.m. I spent the next hour walking around the parking lot and pacing back and forth in front of the terminal, keeping myself warm and awake, watchful while Keith slept. I knew that I would sleep on the flight. As tired as I was, though, when 5 a.m. came, I felt refreshed. I was very grateful when the doors were unlocked and we could move back into the warm.

That morning, as we watched people arrive on flights, pick up luggage and then stay in the terminal, we began to get a little nervous as to whether or not we would be chosen for the flight to Miramar. There were only a two scheduled flights departing that day. One of them was full of soldiers about to deploy. The other was the flight we wanted to board. We could only wait and see.

We conversed with all sorts of people in terminals on this trip. This day is no different. Today's traveling family hails from Hawaii, consisting of a mom, her two teen sons and pre-teen daughter. Dad is on deployment and they are on their way to California to pick up their car that has been in storage for a year. They will drive to visit family in Alabama and finally head to the Northeast to tour colleges that the older son is interested in attending.

Mrs. de la Cruz home-schools her children and is very proud of the fact that the older son, Ej (Ephrain Jr.), ran for city council as a Republican in Hawaii at age 18 and received 1,000 votes on his first attempt for office. The colleges he chose to investigate are in or near Washington, D. C. so that he can intern for a legislator.

Keith and I were pretty impressed by his demeanor, his knowledge of political issues, and his awareness of the impact that all of his personal decisions would make in a political arena. Ej remarked that he feels that if someone aspires to the highest office in the land, as he does, they need to start preparing for that quest when they are as young as fourteen years of age.

Ej gave me business cards and we became Facebook friends. I was glad to meet the young man who plans to run for President sometime soon after 2028. I hope I'm around to see it. (Note: Sadly, we learned that Ej de la Cruz died in a motorcycle accident on Christmas Eve, 2015 in Seoul, Korea. He would have made a great president.)

Ej's younger brother, Ethan, is quite impressive, too. Much quieter than his politician brother, he plans on a career of military service so that he'll be a major part of his brother's cabinet after his election.

Roll call came went off without a hitch. There were plenty of seats available and no one was left behind. Keith and I were cautious about getting too excited about being in the plane until we were actually in the air. I settled down to nap and slept most of the way to Miramar.

MCAS MIRAMAR, CALIFORNIA

Once there, we were in the same pinch that we found at Lewis-McChord. While there was a flight to Hickam Air Force Base in Hawaii the next morning, the terminal would be closing almost immediately and wouldn't reopen until at least 8 a.m. Saturday morning. The closest USO is at San Diego International Airport, fifteen miles away. As we sat outside pondering our options, watching the sun lowering in the sky, a taxi pulled up and Ej and his mom came out to meet the driver. As the cab drove away, Ej told us that he was staying at Miramar with his siblings while mom went to San Diego International to pick up a rental car. I wished aloud that we could have shared the taxi with her.

The teenager immediately pulled out his phone and walked toward the terminal. The taxi, half a block away, pulled a U-turn. Ej came over to us and said they were coming back to get us. Wow! I am amazed at how many times people said yes to us when they could have said no or ignored us. We were being greatly blessed! On top of that, when we arrived at the rental car station, the shuttle to the terminal was just boarding. Perfect timing again!

Six o'clock Friday night at San Diego International buzzes! So many people were coming and going. The warm ocean breezes, mixed with the elation of finishing one more leg of the trip, and counting the blessings that had been bestowed upon us, evoked an almost tangible sense of well-being in me. I felt my steps to the USO were light and agile. There was no weight on my shoulders save the carry-on bag with pillows and jackets.

The young lady behind the desk at the USO in San Diego was matter of fact as she spoke to the young sailor in front of us. She was explaining to him that the duty driver had already left on his last run for the day and that he would probably have to stay until morning. He was concerned that he was to report in by tomorrow evening and would not have a way to get to his ship. You can tell that she is military by her bearing. We found out later that she was indeed an active duty sailor who volunteered at the USO during most of her free time. You could also tell that it gave her great pleasure to serve.

We had food, showers and a place to sleep that night and were very comfortable. When they closed at midnight, the volunteers brought out mats, pillows and blankets for those of us who needed them. Although lights were on in the lobby of the USO, we all quieted down quickly and got some much needed sleep. When volunteers reopened the doors at 6 a.m., we were on our feet and ready to go.

We caught a bus right outside the USO. We only had to transfer once, then had about a mile walk back to the base, but the weather was good, and we were refreshed, so it wasn't difficult.

Inside the gate, we stopped at McDonald's for a quick breakfast. At the counter, I overheard a couple talking about picking up food for the flight, so I asked if they were going to the passenger terminal. They were, and were happy to have us ride along. We were all catching the same flight to Hickam Air Force Base in Hawaii and there were plenty of seats.

After already spending over a week on the road, it was nice to finally make it out of the states and closer to our destination.

HICKAM AIR FORCE BASE, HAWAII

When we arrived at Hickam that evening, there were quite a few people in the terminal. Not knowing how long they had been there or where they were going was a little disconcerting. We checked at the desk and learned that there were no flights to Japan or anywhere else for that matter on that particular night and nothing scheduled at all until tomorrow afternoon. The staff on the desk were not particular helpful and at times almost seemed as though they dreaded seeing any of us walking toward the desk. They peppered answers with "as I told you before" and "again" and "one more time," they made us feel that we were an inconvenience to them rather than the reason they had a job.

We had a new traveling partner now, a young lady named Victoria who lives in San Diego and was going to visit her husband in Kadena, Okinawa, Japan. We were all pretty hungry after the long flight so she and I took the free base shuttle, the last of the day, over to the commissary. It was less than a mile away, but we had no idea where we were going or we would have walked. Keith stayed with the luggage. His reward was an extra Snickers bar.

We decided to get a room for the night, and so did Victoria. One of the airmen behind the desk was getting off shift after we ate and was gracious enough to give the three of us a ride to the visitor's quarters. We learned that visitor's quarters are on the Pearl Harbor Base, rather than Hickam, which was quite a distance.

The room at the Navy Gateway Inn at Pearl was very pleasant. The weather is such that air conditioning is not required. We were on the eighth floor and with our windows and shutters open, could feel the ocean breezes. We slept well.

SUNDAY, SEPTEMBER 23

I woke up feeling wonderful that Sunday morning, ready to continue our journey. My first action, even before getting out of bed or waking Keith, was to check Facebook for the most recent updates to Hickam's schedule. Much to my dismay, the Sea-Tac daily report was the first thing on the list of Space-A announcements. There had been 45 seats on the flight to Misawa that morning, and only 35 were filled.

I cried. I cried as quietly as I could. I cried because I didn't have the good sense to stay put. I cried because I knew that Keith was having a difficult time, feeling like we were getting the runaround at every turn. I cried because I wanted to see our daughter.

My crying woke Keith. When I told him the reason for the tears, he lifted the burden from my shoulders and reminded me that he didn't want to just sit in Seattle, either. We made the decision together to try to find a quicker way. It was done and it was okay. Let's move on. I started focusing on the fact that we were in Hawaii!

Living out of suitcases is not all that hard if you have the bags organized, but ours were getting to be a mess. I spent the next couple of hours doing laundry and reorganizing our bags. Then I called Victoria. She was ready to go. We walked four blocks to the bus stop for the base shuttle. When we got to the terminal, it was nearly 11 a.m.

The E6 on duty that morning was much nicer than the people we encountered the night before and we told him so. There were flights scheduled that afternoon to the states, but nothing to Japan. There was, however, a flight to Guam on Monday morning. That would get us closer still. A quick check of the internet showed that flights were often scheduled from Andersen Air Force Base in Guam to Kadena Air Base, Okinawa.

We waited all that day, making new friends, all of us hoping that something would break through to allow us to travel. Then we learned that a typhoon was threatening the Pacific and was the reason for the flight schedule changes and cancellations. Sunday became Monday.

Monday, September 24

When roll call was finally called for the flight to Guam, there were only ten seats available. We were really excited that Victoria made it onto the flight. As I helped her get her bags, I shook my head at Keith, indicating that we were not going to make it on this one.

Then I heard the lady call another name, but I couldn't make it out as I went back toward the desk with Victoria's luggage. I didn't see anyone move. When I got to the desk, I asked if she had called our name. We made it! We were the last two chosen for the flight!

Or did we?

Our bags were scanned. We were standing in line for them to be weighed and to receive boarding passes when another employee came out from the offices to the counter. "We just got a call that there are four more active duty that are on their way."

The airman weighing the bags looked at us, looked at him and looked back at us again. I held my breath. "They're not here. We're going to go ahead and check these people in."

We DID make it!

There were only ten of us. We'd met four of our fellow travelers already; Victoria, the young military wife who shared luggage watch with us; Jenna, another wife on her way back to Kadena; Daniel, a sailor on leave; Wes, a young sailor in the middle of a transfer from the Navy base at Guam. We were all very glad to be going to Guam. At least, today, we were.

ANDERSEN AIR FORCE BASE, YIGO, GUAM

TUESDAY, SEPTEMBER 25

Datelines being what they are, we arrived in Guam on Tuesday afternoon.

When we got through Customs in Guam, Keith found himself out in the smoking area with Wes, discussing plans for leaving the terminal. I stayed inside, checking on flights for the next leg.

When they came back in, Keith told me that Wes offered us his room at the barracks, but it was nearly forty miles away. Daniel had reservations at a hotel in the middle of Guam. Jenna rented a car and she and Victoria were sharing a room off base. We all just needed a way to get where we were going.

Wes called the Navy base and the duty driver picked four of us up at the terminal. After dropping Daniel at his hotel, we stopped at the USO nearby, just to check it out. It was amazing. They were serving a hot meal of chili over rice and barbecued ribs. They have a very large facility but they were only open until 10 p.m. After filling our bellies, we went to the Navy base.

True to his word, Wes gave us his room. We went to bed immediately, even though it was only about 7 p.m. When I woke up at midnight, Wes was still up, hanging out with friends in the courtyard. He took me to the nearby club to try to get Wi-Fi on my phone, but I was unable to make a connection so I went back to bed, leaving him with friends at the club.

Wednesday, September 26

Keith and I both woke up at 4:30 a.m. and found Wes sleeping on the floor in the anteroom. Keith woke him and sent him to his bed and we went out for a walk, covering only about two or three square blocks. As the sun started lighting the dark sky, sailors were coming out of buildings all around us in PT clothes. A new day was beginning.

We went back to the room, left Wes his room key, picked up our bags and started our hike. We knew how far it was back to Andersen's terminal, so there was no question that we were going to hitchhike. A small pickup stopped when we were only about two blocks from the barracks.

There are two Navy bases on Guam. We were on the base that was the farthest south. The young man who picked up us was a diver, only going to the next base, a few miles farther north. He left us on the main road near the gate to that base.

We had another ride within about 100 yards of being dropped off. Our next ride was a man named Tony. Tony took us several more miles, letting us out at a main intersection.

Getting a ride from there was a bit harder, as there was no shoulder for a car to pull off. If someone was going to stop for us, they would have to pull into a parking lot, completely off the road. We probably walked about 200 yards with several hundred cars passing us before a vehicle pulled over.

Before we got in the car, he asked where we were headed. After Keith responded, he said that he could take us farther up the road, but not all the way to Anderson. He started asking us questions about where we were going, and where we were from. Keith seemed very comfortable with the conversation, but I was a little nervous about sharing the many details he did. Then Keith started asking him questions, too. He was born in the states, but had been raised in Guam. He left there for a time and had been back for eleven years. He told us that his father had been in the Navy. He also told us that the only reason that he stopped to pick us up was because he saw Keith's Vietnam Veteran ball cap.

I began to get more comfortable as he talked about himself and about Guam, but it seemed as though the ride was getting long for only taking us part way. Then I noticed signs indicating that the base was only five miles away. He had decided to take us all the way to Andersen's main gate. He pulled into the parking lot at the visitor's center and got out to help us get our bags from the back of the SUV.

I'm sorry that I can't take you all the way to the terminal, but I'm a civilian and can't get on base without a pass." He gripped Keith's hand in his two hands. "I want to thank you very much for your service, sir," he said, leaving paper in Keith's grip. "Please take this token for your trip."

Keith felt the bill and stuffed in his pocket without looking at it. "Thank you, sir, for your kindness in giving us a ride." They nodded to each other and the man returned to his car. We waved and thanked him again as he waved from his open window. Keith took the bill from his pocket, looked at it, and stuffed it right back in.

"He was very nice to give us a ride all the way here," I said to Keith as the car pulled away.

Keith said softly, unbelief written on his face, "He gave us a hundred dollars!"

"Oh, wow! Thank you, Lord!" was all that could reach my lips. I was almost in tears with gratitude. We had already spent way more on rooms than planned and this was $2 more than we spent.

As we presented our ID cards at the gate, we got another surprise. An officer, dressed in civilian clothes, walked up to the marine who was checking our identification. "Do they have ID cards?" the man asked as he strode confidently.

The marine apparently recognized him and straightened his posture. "Yes, sir," he replied.

The man spoke directly to Keith. "Are you going to the PAX terminal? I saw your bags and thought you might need a ride."

"Yes, sir, we are," Keith answered him, immediately recognizing the man's command presence.

"Then hop on in. I'll take you there. It's quite a distance from here and will take too long for you to walk it in this heat," as the man lead us to his car. Keith asked him if there was someplace near the terminal to eat. "There's a Burger King about three blocks from the terminal. I can take you there if that's where you'd rather go." He did. On that five minute ride, Keith explained that we were on our way to visit our daughter in Japan and we learned that the man had been stationed in Guam for most of his career and loved it there.

While the air was a bit humid and the temperature was reaching into the 80s, I didn't care too much. I was just glad to be one flight away from Japan.

The kindness and concern of these and other folks along the way was amazing. Sadly, rudeness and disdain met us as well, but only in Guam.

As a military retiree's wife, I have been to or lived on over thirty military bases in forty years. I have also worked in customer service in some capacity, from cashier to business owner, for much of my life. I have never experienced such treatment as we received in Guam, and we weren't the only people who had the same perception. I was truly grateful that my husband and daughter served in the Navy rather than the Air Force because of the impression that these people were conveying.

I have made customer complaints before. I had been on the receiving end of a complaint only twice in my life. I do not take complaints lightly nor do I make them without foundation. I taught my own employees that no matter how bad it looks, a problem with a customer can usually be solved with kind words and actually caring about their problem, searching for a solution.

Obviously, when traveling Space-A, you are subject to some discomfort. We were already getting used to that. We were not, however, used to being spoken to rudely. There were quite a few instances of this in Guam.

Our real problems started when the staff there told us that we could not fly into Misawa. Although there were not flights scheduled to Misawa at the time, I explained that I had looked into the regulations on the State Department web site, and, though there were restrictions, we could fly into Misawa, provided we stayed on the base until Customs arrived to check us into the country.

Everyone, from the Master Sergeant in charge down to the lowest ranking airmen, told us that we, absolutely, could not fly into Misawa without a Standard of Forces Agreement (SOFA) stamp on our passports, and the only way to get a SOFA stamp is to live in Japan. Therefore it would be impossible to go to Misawa. (See IMPORTANT LINKS for the January, 2015 International Security Advisory Board Report on Status of Forces Agreements. This explains the SOFA stamp and its relevance.)

That was that. We had been in Guam overnight and there were no flights to Misawa yet, anyway. I tried to get on the State Department website, but the Foreign Clearance Guide, which is where I found the original information, is blocked in overseas locations, so I couldn't access it to get my proof. We were stuck, so we decided to make the best of it, waiting for a flight that would go anywhere in Japan. We would make our way to Misawa from there.

Earlier in the day, Daniel and Jenna told us that Victoria took a commercial flight to Guam. She was on a very tight schedule and couldn't wait for the flights to open up. Jenna and Daniel both decided, too, that if they were not able to get out that day, they would get find commercial flights as well.

Nine Marines came into the terminal that morning, also on standby to go to Kadena. They had settled in somewhat, anticipating a long wait for a flight, as we were. That afternoon, four of them were playing Spades and Keith was standing nearby watching them, kibitzing. Finally, one of the young Marines, Micah Crowell, picked up the bait.

"If you think you can do better, sir, we'll be glad to challenge you to a game." Young Crowell grinned as he stepped right into the trap.

"Jackie," Keith turned and called to me. I was reading a book, about ten feet away. "They want to challenge us at Spades!"

"Done and done!" I exclaimed. I was ready for a change of activity. "You boys must know that this is a mistake, right?" I looked at the four sitting cross-legged on the floor.

"No, ma'am," said Crowell. "We can surely beat you."

Keith and I have been playing Spades together since before our wedding thirty-six years before. We knew the game well and knew each other's playing style almost perfectly. This was going to be a hoot!

It was. After finishing the game they were already playing, Crowell and his partner came over to us with the cards. We sat on the floor in the middle of chairs and baggage carts. People we had shared terminals with in both Hawaii and now Guam, watched with interest as we started off by discussing the rules.

Keith was counting the cards. “Why are there jokers in here? You don’t use jokers in Spades.”

“We do,” the partner spoke up. “They’re the highest cards in the deck and you take out the deuces of hearts and clubs.”

“What?” We were curious, but not convinced. They went on to explain how the jokers worked and the deuces came out and how you score and all sorts of oddball rules. We were not going down that road. “You mean you really don’t know how to win fair and square without all those variations? You don’t know how to play Spades, just Spades?” They agreed to play without embellishments: no jokers, no nil, no ten-for-two, and minimum bid of four per team.

Sonja Joyner told us later that, while watching us get ready to play, she had laughed and told her husband, Ralph, that we obviously had been playing together for years and were going to stomp those guys. She was right.

People were watching, laughing, and enjoying the show as we took the youngsters down a notch. Their OIC stopped by our “table” and told us that he’d advised them not to play because they would be sorely up against it, but they didn’t take his advice. Now they were suffering. Near the end of the game, Crowell admitted that we had them, but that they could surely win if they were able to play by the rules that they were accustomed to. We soundly outscored them, over 500 to less than 100. We offered them a rematch later, but they shipped out before the opportunity presented.

Jenna and Daniel left us on Wednesday. They'd had it. There was a flight to Kadena with 65 seats. It seemed we would all be able to board, but at the last minute, a Japanese Air Defense Unit arrived and was given all seats. Daniel and Jenna found commercial flights to Kadena for less than $350 and were happy to pay it. They both gave us their addresses or phone numbers. Daniel told us that, when we got to Kadena, we should call and he would take us out to dinner. We had been in two terminals with him for several days and we would miss talking with him.

On Wednesday afternoon, a flight to Misawa Japan came up on the board with a 7:40 a.m. Thursday roll call. There was also a flight listed to Atsugi, Japan slated for Thursday evening. I went back to the desk again, this time finding a civilian attendant who actually listened when I spoke. I explained to him that I had checked the Foreign Clearance Guide and he actually looked SOMETHING up in a book on the desk. He said that there were two parts to the directions and that one seemed to contradict the other. The Master Sergeant came to the desk and said that there is a large fine for sending people to Misawa without SOFA stamps and that he would not pay that $20,000 fine for anyone. He would not even look at the FCG.

I messaged our daughter to find out if she had any contacts in Misawa that might be able to help us get this sorted out. She made some calls, and had people for us to stay with on base until the necessary procedures were followed with Customs, but couldn't find anyone to help us out from there.

Thursday, September 27

Next morning, I was desperate. The people at the desk were still saying no. Roll call came and went with empty seats, but they did not call our names. I called the terminal at Misawa and spoke with the airmen there regarding the rules for entry into the country. Airman L___ said that we could come into Misawa as long as we did not leave the base without having been stamped into the country by Japanese Customs. I asked if he would speak with people from Guam and explain what must be done. He said that he'd be glad to. I gave the airman at the desk the phone number and explained that Misawa would be waiting for the call.

Time was ticking. The selectees for the Misawa flight were already in the departure area when an airman came to us with a document. A paragraph near the center of the page was highlighted in blue. The highlighted portion was an instruction regarding entry into NAF Atsugi. The gist of the Foreign Clearance Guide instruction1 is that if Non-SOFA personnel come into Atsugi, they must remain on base at their own expense until either Japanese Immigrations officials come to the base or a Navy escort takes them to Yokohama to be in-processed. He told us that he spoke with Misawa and we could indeed go into a SOFA only designated terminal, but we would have to stay on base until immigration came to the base. He handed me the paper and went back to his station behind the desk.

As I scanned the lines, my eyes were drawn two paragraphs above. II.E.f reads "Non-SOFA personnel arriving at Misawa AB after 1530 are restricted to the Base overnight until Japanese immigration officials open for business the next day." Three quick steps took me to the desk where I pointed it out to the airman.

"See? See this? This says that we can go into Misawa, but we have to stay on base to wait for immigration. We already have a place to stay on base. This is what I have been telling you all this time!" My frustration could not be hidden.

His eyebrows raised a little as he read the directive. "Looks like you might be right," he said.

"Then we can still get on the Misawa flight, right?"

"I'm afraid not, ma'am. They're already gone." No words could have been crueler at that moment. I turned away and cried for the third time. We were not on an adventure anymore. We were in hell.

Keith is a very staunch believer in following the chain of command when there is a problem. Some of my antics frustrate him a bit, but he tolerates it when it doesn't cause trouble for anyone. On this occasion, however, even HE was ready to tear his hair out. We talked for a while about what to do next. Keith decided it was one of those rare instances where it would be okay to jump the chain.

As we walked to Base Headquarters, we relived the chain of events that brought us to this moment. The lack of respect from several individuals behind the counter made it easy to put them on the chopping block, if necessary. The most important aspect, though, was that the rule book was right there in front of them and nobody bothered to open it until it was too late. We missed the only flight to Misawa in a week.

We were a little intimidated as we were escorted into the office of the Command Chief Master Sergeant, but the fear disintegrated as he welcomed us into his office. He listened carefully, asking few questions as Keith recounted events leading to this meeting. He glanced briefly at the pages we held from the Foreign Clearance Guide.

"This really is not my area of expertise," he began, "but let me make a phone call or two and I'll find somebody who can sort this out for you."

"Thank you, sir," Keith answered. "Would you like us to step out while you're on the phone?"

"Not at all," the sergeant replied. "This shouldn't take long."

We sat quietly, listening as he made several calls. The last call he made was to a lieutenant at the AMC terminal.

He made small talk for about ten seconds, and then got to work. "Lieutenant, I have a couple here in my office that's trying to go to Misawa. Now, they showed me a paper that was given to them by somebody over there that says that it's okay. I explained to them

that I don't know all the rules and regulations that are involved here, but I know that's your area of expertise, so I'm going to send them over to you to get all this taken care of for them, okay?" Obviously we couldn't hear the other side of the conversation. "Humphrey. That's right. They'll be coming over to see you in a bit. You'll be there, right?" The last question sounded more like a command than a request. He thanked the LT for his help and smiled our way as he hung up the phone.
We stood and both shook the sergeant's hand as he promised us that this lieutenant was the best person to help us with our plight.

We left his office and walked back out into the sunshine, feeling on top of the world.

At least we would be able to go to Japan tonight. We could go to Atsugi.

When we got back to the terminal, we went straight to the desk and asked for the lieutenant. The airman nodded toward the group of five or six staff members, huddled with an officer we had not seen before. Several members of the group spotted our arrival and the group quickly dispersed. The officer we had not recognized came up to us immediately, with the master sergeant close behind. "Mr. Humphrey?" he asked as he held his hand out to shake Keith's hand.

"Yes, sir," Keith's tone was matter-of-fact.

"I am Lt. D. MSgt. M. here is going to help you with your problem." He was not going to get involved, so he handed us back over to the man who said that he would not pay a $20,000 fine for sending us into Japan without SOFA stamps.

"I am sorry. I understand your problem, but we cannot send you into Misawa without a SOFA stamp," MSgt. M. played the same song we had heard before. "You can only be put on certain flights due to Japanese immigration laws."

"That's not what the clearance guide says," I spoke up. "Your people are the ones who actually gave us the copy of the regs. It says right here that we can go, but have to stay on base to wait for immigration people to show, which is what we've wanted to do all along." I was beginning to get frustrated all over again. He took the pages and scoured the area that I pointed out. While he was reading, the E4 who had given us nothing but nasty remarks and dirty looks strode confidently to his side, waiting to hear his decision. "Well, it looks as though you may be right. We'll check this out." He indicated to her where he found the information.

"What? They have to stay on the plane until immigration comes?" she whined as if she would be the one to babysit us.

"No," he answered. "It just means they have to stay on base until immigration shows up."

"Which is what we wanted to do anyway," I reminded him. "So, that means we can get on the flight to Atsugi this evening, then, right?" I was more than ready to leave Guam and if we had to stay on the Navy base at Atsugi for a couple of days, so be it.

"Let me call Atsugi and make sure, but if I read this right, we should be able to make this work," he assured us. I wasn't as confident as I was hopeful. "I should have an answer for you within an hour or so.

Although it seemed like these activities had already taken all day, it was only about 11:30 in the morning by now, so Keith and I decided to walk to Subway at the BX for lunch. That would take us at least an hour.

When we got back to the terminal, MSgt. M. came out to us right away, FCG page in his hand. "I have good news and some not so good news, depending on how you look at it," he said. "First, though, I am very sorry that it took this long to figure all this out. We are learning the rules, too, and we don't have it all down pat. The rule preventing Non-SOFA persons from boarding certain flights is fairly new. Apparently, it has arisen because people were not waiting on the bases for the immigration people to come. There is a big fine to the Air Force if we send people into Japan without proper documentation." He seemed pretty sincere. "I'm also sorry that we didn't get this done before you missed the Misawa flight today. There is another flight scheduled to Misawa on Saturday."

I let out a big sigh.

"We spoke with Atsugi," he continued, "and they said that you could actually fly into there on this evening's flight. However, there is a catch." We waited, wondering what could be so difficult about this decision. "When you get there, you have to turn in your ID cards and passports to Japanese authorities. You will be under armed guard until you are taken to Yokohama's immigration office, and you must pay all expenses. They will be in charge of you until you are stamped in to the country.

"Yikes!" I thought. Keith and I looked at each other and waited.

"Did you want to go to Atsugi, then?" asked the MSgt.

"Yes," we both answered, nodding our heads. We didn't have to think about it.

As the MSgt. walked away, though, we did think about it. We went outside, away from people and started talking.

"I don't know about you, but I didn't just get red flags when he was talking. I saw flares!" Keith was very concerned that we may have made the wrong decision. "I have a little bit of a problem with giving up my passport and my ID card in a foreign country. Maybe I've seen too many movies, but we could get off that plane and never be heard from again!"

"I've seen the same movies," I agreed. "Armed guard doesn't necessarily scare me. Military police carry weapons. But giving up all of our identification scares me to death." I wasn't kidding.

"Then we have to wait, either for another flight to Kadena or Yokota, or for the Saturday flight to Misawa," Keith decided. "At least they'll let us on it this time."

We went back inside and talked with Ralph and Sonja Joyner. They had come on the flight with us from Hawaii and were waiting for a flight to Kadena. We became good friends with the Joyners in Guam. They were a home-schooling family, too. Mom Sonja was very aware of our plight and kept encouraging me that God would work things out for us. Their family had all the clearances necessary to get back to Kadena. "They said that we can go to Atsugi, but we have to be under armed guard and give our ID cards and passports to the Japanese until they take us to the immigration office in Yokohama," Keith explained. Ralph raised his eyebrow and cocked his head a little.

As they listened to us explain the requirements and our fears, Ralph shook his head. "I wouldn't give those up. Something doesn't sound exactly right here," he said. Their misgivings, coupled with our own, solidified our decision.

We asked at the desk for the MSgt. When he came out of his office, he was very friendly, and asked what he could do for us. We believe that since he thought we were going to leave that night, it seemed as though he was having a better day. He was ready for us to stop making waves.

"We appreciate that you have gone to the trouble of contacting Atsugi to make arrangements for us to go there," Keith spoke humbly, "but in light of the requirements to give up ID cards and passports, we have decided to pass on this flight and wait for another to Japan, whether it be Kadena, Yokota, or Misawa."

"I understand," he said. "I wouldn't want to go under those conditions, either."

As disappointed as we were, at least we knew that we finally had the right information and that the Air Force believed us.

That night was $1 night at Gecko Bowl, the base bowling alley. Games, shoes, and beer were $1 each. Several of our Marine friends were going and asked us if we'd like to join them. It was a welcome respite from sitting in the terminal, waiting, waiting, and waiting some more.

FRIDAY, SEPTEMBER 28

The Joyner family was the only group to catch a flight on Friday. There was a flight to Yokota that only had room for four passengers and there are four Joyners; Ralph, Sonja, Jacob and McKenzie. Although they live in Kadena, they were unwilling to wait for a direct flight to Kadena, so they decided to go to Yokota and make their way to Kadena by train. Before they boarded their flight, Sonja encouraged us to let them know through Jacob's Facebook page if we ended up in Kadena and had a layover. They offered us beds to sleep in and a home-cooked meal.

By late Friday morning, the Saturday Misawa flight slipped to Sunday morning, so we knew there were at least forty-eight more hours to wait for a ride to Misawa. I talked Keith into renting bicycles for $5 a day. It was nice enough to be outside, but we'd had our fill with walking to the Fitness Center, the BX, Burger King, the Commissary and the Shoppette. Everything but the Commissary was at least a half mile away. Making five or six trips out per day was getting really old.

SATURDAY, SEPTEMBER 29

While we only had them for one day, we sure did get a lot accomplished. We went to every one of those places at least once. We did laundry, went for showers and naps at the Fitness Center, and rode to the BX just to explore. By the time we turned the bikes in late Saturday afternoon, our bottoms were sore, but our feet were grateful to have a break in the walking.

We walked back from turning the bikes in to find our expectations crumble once again. The Sunday morning Misawa flight slipped to Monday and then was later cancelled. This was getting quite discouraging again.

Sunday, September 30

By now, nearly everyone still left in the small terminal knows our plight. We've been here for six days. We could have gone three days ago, but terminal personnel would not listen to our explanations until it was too late to catch Thursday's flight. At that point, the fact that we were right about anything made little difference to us. We wanted to go to Japan! That's all that mattered.

Terrible tension started building between Keith and I. We certainly weren't mad at each other. We were both sorely disappointed in our situation. I started blaming myself again for a number of things. I shouldn't have suggested leaving Sea-Tac and missing the following Sunday's flight. I shouldn't have pushed to start this trip until we had more money to spend. I shouldn't have packed as many clothes. I didn't plan this very well.

Nearly every conversation we had evolved into an argument. Every complaint that Keith had was an indictment. TSA rules state that you cannot sleep on the floor of the terminal under any circumstances. We had to sleep in chairs almost every night. Every bone in both of our bodies was screaming that we needed restful sleep. We were weary and extremely on edge.

Monday, October 1

Finally, on day 8 in Guam, we were on a flight to Kadena, but only after another delay.

An officer's wife, who had evacuated from Kadena before the typhoon, arrived for the flight wearing sandals. Her bags were checked and already on the plane before it was noticed that she was wearing open-toe shoes. Despite the fact that the terminal announcement recordings repeat the prohibition of this apparel numerous times per hour, all boarding was nonetheless delayed while a friend went to her own base housing and returned with a pair of athletic shoes.

KADENA AIR BASE, OKINAWA

When we touched down in Kadena, it was about around 7 p.m., and nearly dark. Keith and I waited while all of the other passengers were checked in at the desk Then we were taken in the terminal's van to the immigration office in Kadena. The driver told us that the office closed at 10 p.m., but it wasn't too far away, so we were there in plenty of time. The gentleman behind the desk checked and made copies of our ID cards and passports, then stamped our passports that we were in the country. The airman took us back to the terminal and we were free to go. We were finally in Japan.

I had messaged Sonja through Jacob's Facebook page that we were there. She picked us up about ten minutes later with hugs all around as we reunited with our friend. After a quick trip to the Exchange Food Court for fried chicken dinner, we were on our way to the Joyner home in Kadena, Okinawa, Japan.

Ralph and the kids were genuinely happy to see us. I got an extra big hug from McKenzie, who seemed to become attached to me as early as our first real conversation in Guam. Jacob, being older and more reserved about such things, still couldn't help smiling a lot. The family fussed over us so that it was a little embarrassing, but heartening at the same time. We had been through the mill and it wasn't over yet, but here was a pleasant break in the drama.

McKenzie gave up her bedroom so that Keith and I could rest comfortably. It was very nice to be able to sleep through the night without the lights on, without recorded announcements blaring every ten minutes, and without unhappy children crying at all hours. We slept in such peace until about 6 a.m.

Tuesday, October 2

As you've probably recognized by now, my morning routine in the states was to check the Facebook page of the terminal we were in (or near) immediately upon waking up, so that I would know how fast we had to get moving to be able to get to the next leg. Outside the U.S., though, I had to call the terminals to get the information.

That morning, I leisurely postponed my call so that I could visit with Ralph for a few minutes before he left for work. After that, a cup of tea in hand, I called the Kadena terminal. They had posted a flight to Misawa that morning and roll call was at 7:40 a.m. It was 7:15 a.m. and Keith was still in bed.

I ran up the stairs, burst into the room, ran over to the bed and tapped his arm. "Keith," I stage whispered, "There's a flight to Misawa this morning. Roll call in twenty minutes." I was hurriedly stuffing clothes into whatever bag was handy. I didn't care how they fit. I could fix that later.

Keith threw on his clothes, grabbed shoes, socks, and two bags, and hurried down the stairs. By the time we got to the bottom of the stairs, Sonja was speaking. "I called them back to let them know that you were on the way and they said that there are no seats released on this flight." Our disappointment was obvious in the drop of our shoulders and the slow setting down of our bags.

"Well, at least we're all packed up," I said, as brightly as I could muster. "And we're wide awake. Jacob, what other flights are listed on Facebook today?" There was one to Osan, Korea with four tentative seats and one to Yokota, Japan with only six seats.

"I have a phone call to make first. Then I'll take you to the terminal and if you don't get out today, you just call me. I'll come back to get you so you stay here again tonight." Sonja was very definite about how this was going to play out.

"Thank you, Sonja. You are such a good friend already," I said. "We greatly appreciate your hospitality."

Sonja made her call then wrote down several phone numbers for getting in touch with her in case we needed her. Then we hugged the children, loaded our bags into the car and off we went. We were back in the Kadena terminal that morning by 9 a.m.

There were art displays everywhere throughout the terminal. Colorful paintings, fans and other decorative items graced every turn. This was undoubtedly the most beautifully decorated airport I'd ever seen.

Kadena's Facebook page told the whole story for that day. We learned from the agents at the desk that the only flights out were the two mentioned to Osan and Yokota. We stayed at the terminal anyway, just in case another flight was written into the schedule.

We did what little exploring there was to do in this average-sized AMC terminal, and then went into the small USO annex. I found a new book to read. Keith watched the end of an old movie. After about thirty minutes of checking flight schedules, I found that Osan had a flight to Misawa on the very next day. The flight to Osan from Kadena had room for four passengers and only two had signed up.

The Air Force customs office airman was very helpful. He explained that if we went to Osan we would have to be stamped out of Japan first. To do that, we would have to go back to the Japanese Immigration Office where we were stamped in the night before. I asked if there was a bus or any government transportation that would allow us to get there and back on time.

No, he said, but advised that we should not get stamped out unless we were actually chosen for the flight, so we waited for roll call.

We were selected! We had our boarding passes in hand and it was just about noon. I called Sonja and explained what had happened. She dropped everything and came to take us to the immigration office. We arrived there at 12:45. Keith and I jumped from the van and ran to the door, only to find that the door was locked for lunch until 1 p.m. We walked back to the van and told Sonja the situation.

I went back to the door. I don't know what I was expecting to find. I only knew that I should be at the door. I peered in through the blinds and saw a man in the office eating his lunch. Then I noticed a sign on the door. "If door is locked, passengers and crew members, please ring bell." I looked at Keith, decided that meant us because we were passengers and touched the button.

The man strode across the floor quickly and opened the door. I showed him our boarding passes and passports. "Can you help us?" I asked.

"Come in," he said, as he waved us into the office.

He took our passports, ID cards and boarding passes, making copies of all. As he inspected the passports, he pointed out that we had just signed in the day before. He looked at us quizzically, shaking his head. He stamped our passports with the appropriate information and handed them back. We were out of the door before 1 p.m. Now we just had to be back at the terminal by 1:30 p.m. Sonja's knowledge of the area got us back in plenty of time. We thanked and hugged her again before she drove away.

When we got back to the terminal, we were all smiles, knowing that we were only two steps from Misawa. A number of people had come into the terminal, waiting for the Yokota flight. By the count, we knew that with only six seats available, we would not have made that flight. We knew that we made the right decision to go to Korea.

The announcement was made for the people with boarding passes to Osan's flight to come to the counter to prepare for boarding. While we were being escorted to the boarding area, an airman from the flight line came to the counter and spoke quietly to the agent. The agent looked up at us, nodding his head, and after a brief pause, walked in our direction.

You cannot imagine the dread the overwhelmed me. I knew, without a word, that something had happened and we were not going on this flight.

"Mr. and Mrs. Humphrey, I'm very sorry, but the crew tells us that they can only take two passengers on this flight," the agent began, "so you will not be able to go on it. They will be bringing your checked bags back out here in a few moments."

"What happened?" I demanded. "We just went to immigration and got stamped out of the country. What now?"

"The customs officer that you spoke with before can help you with that. He isn't in his office now but will be back very shortly," he informed us.

I waited until we had our bags and were seated out in the waiting area before I cried again. This time it wasn't as much for me as it was for what we had put Sonja through just a short time ago. We decided that we were not going to tell her about being bumped from the flight unless we absolutely had no choice.

By now, it was almost time for the roll call for the Yokota flight. Since there were only six seats on this flight and about thirty people waiting for selection, we knew that our chances were slim to none. All of the usual announcements were made regarding footwear and carry-on luggage. This time there was an additional announcement.

"Passengers, please be advised that the aircraft for this flight is a C-12 and you are limited to thirty pounds of checked baggage plus carry on." The terminal quickly quieted as people realized that their bags were not going to meet weight limitations.

Roll call began. One after another, people were sent to the baggage scale to have their luggage weighed. If their luggage qualified them for the flight, they were given boarding passes. If it didn't qualify, some went back to their seats, but most went out the door. Many were turned away. When the final name was called, many of those not selected left the terminal to try another day.

We didn't. We couldn't. We weren't going to call Sonja until we knew for sure there would be no more flights for the day. That wouldn't be until the terminal closed that evening.

Suddenly, the PA system, squealed as it was brought back to life. "May I have your attention, please? The flight to Yokota has released four more seats and we will continue roll call."

They did. Name after name was called and no one answered. They were gone. A family of five was waiting, but there were only four seats. They passed. Another couple answered, but when I saw their luggage, I knew that they would not qualify. I dare not hope that we would get on that flight, but as each name was called and not answered, my hopes starting increasing.

Then they called Ryan. "Yes!" he cried out. "Come on, buddy, we made it!" He grabbed up his small son and headed toward the counter, pulling his small suitcase, with another smaller one on top of it. A young lady trailed slightly behind them, grinning at their good fortune, and carrying a small backpack.

The hope that had suddenly started growing died just as suddenly. There were three of them. Since there were only four seats, we were not going, no matter what. Then I knew that my ears deceived me. "Mr. Humphrey!" was the announcement.

I looked quickly toward the counter. I held up two fingers. "There are two of us," I said from about fifteen feet away. The agent waved us up to the counter. "There are two of us," I explained again. Confused, Keith rose from his seat and grabbed the bags as the man nodded toward the scale.

While we waited for Ryan to have bags weighed boarding passes issued, another woman in uniform came to the counter, picked up the little boy, hugged and kissed him and said goodbye. We couldn't help but overhear her calling herself mommy. Okay, I thought, who's that flying with them?

Seconds later, the first woman held her arms out to the child. "I have to go back to work, Lucas," she told the boy. "I'm really gonna miss you." The boy hugged her distractedly and looked at his dad.

"We'll get on in a minute," his dad answered. "I appreciate all of your help." He shook the woman's hand as she wished him a safe trip. Then she left the terminal.

The picture became clear. There were only two passengers in that group, Ryan and his son, Lucas. Neither of those women would be taking this trip. That left room for Keith and me on this plane. We didn't care how it happened. All we knew was that we were going to Yokota, which is about halfway from Kadena to Misawa, and we were going today. It was Tuesday, October 2. We had been on the road for over two weeks.

It was a cramped, bumpy ride. Who cared? Yokota was less than five hundred miles from Misawa.

YOKOTA AIR BASE, FUSSA-SHI, TOKYO, JAPAN

We arrived at Yokota well after dark and were shuttled to base lodging. More expense for an overnight room was causing cash to dwindle. Our next challenge was to get from Yokota to Misawa. Yokota, Japan is about 500 miles from Misawa, and not too far from Tokyo.

Wednesday, October 3

True to my morning routine, I was up early to do laundry and check flight schedules. Happily, I viewed a flight from Atsugi to Misawa that was not scheduled until 1 p.m. Atsugi was less than three hours away by train, BUT we had to take three different trains to get there. I woke Keith and we left the base by 7:30 a.m.

What we didn't know was that 1) we needed Yen not Dollars to get on the trains, 2) the exchange rate, and 3) that we would have to walk about 2 miles from the train to Atsugi's base.

At one point, as we stood looking at all of the signs written overhead in this language we could not understand, we spotted a young man who was clearly not Asian. I asked if he spoke English. He replied in Japanese, then started to chuckle. "I'm American," he said, "but I've lived here for several years, so I speak the language pretty well. How can I help you?" We explained our plight and he took the time to show us how to read the signs to find the correct train to transfer to.

As we went our way, we were also helped by several ladies who smiled and giggled to each other each time we spoke. I'm sure we were quite amusing to them. One of their group exchanged our cash for yen and who knows if it was right or not. We needed yen to continue.

When we arrived at our destination station, we were more than a little surprised that we accomplished the trip without erring and ending up in the wrong location.

NAF ATSUGI, TATEKAWA, AYASE, JAPAN

After our long trek from the train station to the base, we were relieved that we arrived with more than an hour to spare. The young female sailor at the terminal desk politely advised us that the plane had not arrived yet and that we were the only passengers that signed up for the flight.

We consumed a leisurely lunch at the snack bar in the terminal. When finished, we waited.

At about 1 p.m., two gentlemen came into the terminal from the hangar. One of the men sat in a chair in the waiting room. The other approached the desk and was talking to the young lady at the counter. The next thing I heard was the girl calling my name.

"Mrs. Humphrey, I'm sorry, but they do not have room for you on this plane. It is filled to the weight limit with cargo."

I was getting used to this, but that didn't make it any easier. I went back to my seat a few steps away and sat. Keith had gone out for a walk. I just sat. My heart was heavy and my body was showing it.

The man in the chair saw my distress. "Are you trying to get to Misawa?" he queried.

"Yes," I replied. "Our daughter is stationed there and we've been trying to get there for over two weeks."

"There is a bus that runs up the coast to Misawa on an overnight trip. It takes about eight or nine hours and the cost is pretty reasonable. I've had to take it myself a couple of times and it was comfortable enough."

I brightened. "Where do I catch this bus?"

"You'll have to take the train back toward Tokyo and go to Shinjuku Station. I can help you make the reservations if you have a card to pay for it." By this time, Keith was back from his walk and we were more than willing to accept his help.

The man went to the desk and asked the attendant for the phone. The next thing I knew, he was handing it to me to give the operator our credit card number to secure the reservation for that night's bus ride on the Willer Express.

After the reservation was made, the man gave us directions to the bus station. Keith and I expressed our gratitude for his assistance. The man then asked a few questions about where our daughter was stationed and her rank. He also asked how many yen we had in our possession. After I answered him, he handed me a bill and a piece of paper. "Take this," he said, "and pay me back when you get to Misawa. You'll need plenty of yen for this trip. My name and address on base is on that paper." Obviously of rank, he instructed the attendant to call a duty driver to take us back to the train station, shook Keith's hand, and parted with "See you in Misawa."

We would be there tomorrow!

The train ride to Shinjuku was much more relaxing than the trip earlier that day. Tomorrow!

MISAWA, AOMORI, JAPAN

THURSDAY, OCTOBER 4

We're here! It took three weeks, lots of flexibility, more stamina than we thought we had, but we're here.

Our daughter picked us up at the Misawa bus station at about 8:30 a.m. She dropped us off at her home, less than a mile from Misawa Air Base, and went back to work for the day. We would see her after work. In the meantime, we decided to find our benefactor and repay his loan. Imagine our surprise when we got to his office and found that he was very highly ranked.

We stayed with our daughter in Misawa for a nearly two weeks. We attended the Navy Ball, rode bikes, and enjoyed her friends and co-workers from the base. We dined at a few restaurants, including Kappa Sushi, the conveyor-belt sushi bar. My new favorite dish from Japan was yakisoba. We were also able to have lunch with Jenell and her youngsters, and got to meet her husband, while in Misawa.

On October 13, our sailor daughter took us on a day trip to Towada National Park where we viewed many examples of the Japanese culture. The park is home to the Sculpture of Two Maidens and the beautiful Towada Shinto Shrine. Lake Towada itself is the largest crater lake in Honshu Island and is nearly 1100 feet (327 meters) deep. It was a beautiful blue calm, never hinting that it rested in an active volcano. It's a two hour drive from Misawa AFB, but well worth the trip.

GOING HOME

MISAWA TO HICKAM TO TRAVIS

MONDAY, OCTOBER 15

It was time to go and give our kid her life back. The Patriot Express to Sea-Tac would not be returning to the states for a few days, but a flight to Hawaii was leaving the next day. Rather than take a chance that the PE would be full, we decided to travel back home through Hawaii. Thankfully, getting home was not quite as difficult as getting to Japan.

TUESDAY, OCTOBER 16

Boarding at Misawa went smoothly. Hickam, thought, had no flights to the state for a couple of days. Staying two nights in the terminal at Hickam gave us new friend opportunities. We met Bill and Sandy, pastors from a church in South Carolina and Ed and Nellie from North Carolina. The bulk of our return Space-A trip was spent with these two couples. We walked, talked, laughed, cried, prayed, and ate together for several days. We watched out for each other. Actually, they all watched out for us more than we did for them, as they knew the pitfalls of Space-A travel and were willing to help us avoid them. We are eternally grateful. (Note: We have learned that Ed passed away in October, 2016. We are sure that many are missing him.)

THURSDAY, OCTOBER 18

Finally, a flight to the mainland was available. We flew into Travis Air Force Base, arriving in mid-afternoon. The terminal does not stay open overnight, so we got rooms for the night on base. We had a great meal in the mess, then strolled back to our rooms, enjoying the pleasant California evening air. Sleeping in the terminal at Hickam had been hard on our bodies. We all really needed the rest, so the evening ended very early.

TRAVIS TO TYNDALL TO JACKSONVILLE

Friday, October 19

From Travis AFB, we logged miles to Tyndall Air Force Base, the closest we could get to the east coast. Tyndall is located near Panama City, Florida. Remember that we left our car in Dayton, Ohio? So now we had to find a route that would get us there from Florida. Very few flights ever leave from Tyndall, at least not going anywhere near our destination. There were no flights at all out of Tyndall for the next few days, so alternative transportation was necessary. Our group of six was shuttled off-base as quickly as possible by the staff at Tyndall, preparing to leave for the weekend. From there we caught a taxi to the Panama City Greyhound Station.

We had lived in Jacksonville, Florida for twelve years and had many friends there, so we were pretty sure that we could find a bed and/or a ride to catch a flight going north. Keith and I decided to go to Jacksonville, as we knew we could get a flight up the east coast at some point. Our new friends lived on the east coast, although farther north, so we boarded the bus to Jacksonville together.

Saturday, October 20

Arriving in Jax after 2 a.m. on Saturday morning, Bill and Sandy transferred to another bus and went home to South Carolina. Ed and Nellie were going to visit nearby family and were waiting to be picked up. Keith and I walked around downtown Jacksonville until daylight when the city bus started running. Then we boarded the bus that went to NAS Jax. Once on the bus, I reached our friend, Heather, who lived near the base. She picked us up at the bus stop and took us home, fed us, then drove us to the base terminal.

Once more, there was a delay. We were actually in the air on Saturday afternoon, but the pilot circled back and landed back at NAS Jax due to some mechanical malfunction. We waited a couple of hours, but finally the flight was canceled.

Next available flight was to Charleston, South Carolina on Sunday. So, we went back to Heather's for the night, where we awoke early Sunday morning to a beautiful sunrise.

CHARLESTON, DAYTON AND HOME

SUNDAY, OCTOBER 21

Charleston! Maggie and Johnny lived in Charleston! I emailed a message to Maggie that we were arriving in Charleston that night. Because it was going to be after 9 p.m. when we arrived, we stayed at the terminal that night. They would pick us up in the morning so we could go have lunch together before we flew back out.

MONDAY, OCTOBER 22

As it happened, there were no flights going north from Charleston that day. We were getting a bit desperate to get home, so I checked to see what a rental car would cost. "Thirty dollars a day," the operator said. "Normally, it would be $150 additional to drop the vehicle off in another city. However, I have one that needs to go back to the Dayton, Ohio airport. So the additional drop-off fee is waived."

I couldn't believe my ears. "I'll take it," I said, as soon as she finished speaking. We were driving the rest of the way home! Maggie and Johnny arrived at the terminal just after the call. We greeted each other like old friends. There was plenty of laughter at lunch as we related the stories of our adventure. Too soon, the meal was finished and we were parting again. They took us to

Charleston airport where we picked up the rental car and headed for Ohio.

It was a ten hour drive. We required sleep shortly before we got to Dayton.

TUESDAY, OCTOBER 23

It was dark-thirty when we were ready to hit the road again. We picked up our car from the lot at Wright-Patterson. I followed Keith to the Dayton airport to drop off the rental car. It still wasn't light yet when we turned in the keys.

Last leg of this trip was 435 miles. We were almost giddy as we got closer to home, finally arriving on Wednesday evening.

We had a wonderful time with our daughter. We made many new friends. We learned a lot about Space-A travel. We would do it again. Next time, though, we'll be a little more patient. Patience would have saved us at least two weeks of travel on the way there. But then, we wouldn't have met all of these fine people. Personally, I wouldn't trade any of them.

When you finally take the plunge, be sure to enjoy yourself. Travel is what we make it. It can be a great adventure or a real pain. Make the most of it and you won't feel LOST IN SPACE-A.

TAKEAWAYS

RULES

Getting on the plane is the culmination of following a myriad of rules and regulations that qualify a person to fly any particular Space-A flight. You can get most of this information from Air Mobility Command. Although this is a benefit to us as retirees, there is never a guarantee that you will get on a flight. There are numerous things to consider that will affect your chances for selection when planning your trip.

- ✓ Your category
- ✓ Correct documents
- ✓ Date and time of sign up
- ✓ Time of year
- ✓ Number of seats released
- ✓ Size of aircraft
- ✓ Cargo
- ✓ Baggage

CATEGORY

The starting point is to know your Category. This is the most important information you need to start making your plans. There are six categories of Space-Available Priority. Whether you are an active duty service member on emergency leave, a dependent traveling without your sponsor, or a retiree, your place in line is determined by your travel category. Department of Defense Instruction 4515.13 is the determining protocol. Look up the category definitions in the current revision of the DoD Instruction (currently in Section 4.11) before you start making your plans. Avoid the embarrassment of arriving at the base terminal with your bags packed only to find out that you are not eligible to fly as a Space-A passenger.

Categories as of April, 2017 are as follows:

Category I	Emergency Leave Unfunded Travel
Category II	Accompanied Environmental and Morale Leave
Category III	Ordinary Leave, Relatives, House Hunting Permissive TDY, Medal of Honor Holders, and Foreign Military.
Category IV	Unaccompanied Environmental and Morale Leave
Category V	Permissive TDY (Non-House Hunting), Students, Dependents, Post Deployment /Mobilization Respite Absence, and Others.
Category VI	Retired, Dependents, Reserve, ROTC, NUPOC and Civil Engineer Corps (CEC) members.

DOCUMENTS

For all Space-A travel, you will need to show a minimum of your military ID card. Some terminals may also require a driver license or similar identification. If traveling to another country, you will also need a passport.

Make sure to apply for new or renewal passports at least two or three months before you plan to travel. There is nothing more disappointing than researching and planning to travel outside the country and postponing due to passport delays.

Keep documents in separate places while traveling. This avoids loss of all identification from a single storage location. Should any identification be lost or stolen, report to the U. S. embassy right away.

SIGN UP EARLY!

Once you know your category, the first step in actually qualifying for a flight is signing up with the base that you want to fly FROM. This can usually be accomplished by email, fax, or in person. It almost never can be done over the phone due to privacy issues.

AMC provides a form for email and fax sign up and another for in person sign up.

Space-A passengers for any given flight are chosen from the list of passengers who have signed up to fly from that location and have arrived at the terminal and been marked present for flights leaving on that day. Sign up date does make a difference in your placement on the list of eligible candidates. If five retirees and their spouses are signed up for the six seats available on a flight, passengers will be selected according to who signed up first. This doesn't mean who was at the terminal first on that day. It means who actually sent their email or fax to the terminal saying that they wanted to be on the qualified list to fly at all.

After you have signed up with a terminal, you stay on the list until a) you take a flight from that terminal or b) sixty days after sign-up. After you take a flight from that terminal, you are removed from the list. For example, let's say you are going from Saint Louis, Missouri to Virginia Beach, Virginia and there are no direct flights in either direction. You find that there are a number of flights you can hop from Scott to Andrews to Norfolk and return. As early as possible, you would sign up with the Scott Passenger Terminal and Joint Base Andrews Passenger Terminal to get there and Norfolk or Oceana Passenger Terminal to catch a return flight. You take your flights: Scott to Andrews to Norfolk. To return the same way, you must sign up again at Andrews. You already signed up at Norfolk and/or Oceana to return to Andrews, but since your name was removed from the list on your departure TO Virginia, you must sign up anew.

TIMING

Remember that military flights are for the needs of the military. There are times when many troops need to be moved to various places for various reasons. Reserve trainings often require many seats, especially if a whole unit is traveling together. The timing of the school year is a deciding factor on many routes due to families vacationing. Summer is also the most prevalent time for Permanent

Change of Station (PCS) for troops being reassigned. Seats normally fill very quickly during these times, lessening the likelihood of a Category VI retiree being chosen. It's a wise traveler who contacts the bases they prefer to fly in and out of to check when the least busy season is for that location. Some airfields will only have flights once or twice a month, while others may have up to fifteen flights a day.

How quickly a flight fills up is usually dependent on the time of year, how many in their travel group, and their destination. While most folks may not want to go to Alaska during their children's winter break, quite a few could choose to go to Disney World during Christmas week, making Space-A seats on flights bound for Florida fairly scarce.

Facebook is now a utilized as a fairly accurate resource to get information about what flights are leaving each terminal on any particular day. It also lists the time you have to be there for roll call. However, the listings are only posted a maximum of 72 hours in advance. You will do well to track the terminal schedules for a couple of months to get an idea of where flights are going. You should also call the terminals to get updates as you get closer to your travel date. Terminal Facebook links usually list the terminal phone numbers. Military missions can change in the blink of an eye, causing a flight to leave earlier than expected or not at all. Make the call! You'll be glad you did.

SEAT RELEASE

The number of seats released or made available for Space-A passengers depends on the mission of the particular flight. If it is a training flight, for example, there may not be any seats released or opened for passengers. This goes hand in hand with the number of travelers. If ten seats are released for Space-A passengers on an aircraft to Petersen, Colorado and you, a retiree (Category VI), and your spouse are the only folks who want to hit nearby slopes, you're golden. If there are fifteen others, however, looking for the same ride, your chances of being chosen for this flight could become very slim. Seat release is often found on the Facebook page, but call to verify before leaving for the terminal.

SIZE MATTERS!

If an aircraft only has room for ten passengers, like a C-12, twenty people waiting to go to its destination will not fit on that plane, no matter how much baggage they dump! While most of the larger planes will allow you to check multiple large bags, some smaller craft have very strict size and weight restrictions. Knowing the rules regarding weight can make a big difference in whether or not you are selected for a flight.

For large craft: You can check two pieces of luggage, 70 pounds each, up to 62 linear inches (length plus width height) in size. Family members can share their allowances. Carry-ons have to fit under the seat or in the overhead.

Great, right? You can take half your wardrobe along. BUT, if the only hop available from Point A to Point B is a small craft, the weight limit drastically changes to 30 pounds. What? How can you travel for any length of time with only 30 pounds?

Also, make sure you are not packing prohibited items. Just like TSA at commercial airports, military check-in requires bags to be scanned. And, no, they won't hold your pocket knife or your aerosol hair spray for you to pick up on your way back.

CLOTHING

Wear the right clothing for travel on military flights. It should be tasteful and acceptable in every location that you will board and depart your flights. You should also have layering items, such as sweaters, light jackets, etc. The airplanes can get very cold at high altitudes.

Closed shoes are required: no sandals, high heels, etc.

CARGO

Some of the military planes are huge, like the C-10, so you might wonder why in the world you can't get on that plane when you're the only person in line. If they are carrying sensitive cargo, though, no matter how much or how little, as a civilian, you are probably not going to get on that flight. There are DOD restrictions on how close civilians can get to certain materials, equipment, information, or personnel, and, regardless of how long you were in the service, as a retiree, you are considered a civilian. If you're active duty, your advantage may be affected by your clearance. Remember, Space-A travel is a privilege, not a right.

SMART PHONE APPS

Just about everybody has a smart phone these days and there are several apps that can help make your military travel much easier. Check them out.

- SCOUT Military Discounts writes on their Facebook page, "SCOUT is the most comprehensive mobile app for military discounts & savings with thousands of military discounts." iOS and Android. https://www.scoutmilitary.com/

- Discount Soldier says "Start saving money right now with our extensive list of military discounts." iOS and Android. http://www.discountsoldier.com/

- MyBaseGuide has over 150 Installations listed. Available for iOS and Android. http://mybaseguide.com/page/153/MBG%20App

The next three are my go-to apps for military travel. We don't travel without all three available.

- <u>Base Directory by Military Traveler</u> is my old reliable. I've been able to find small bases all over the country with this app, making it very helpful when looking for base lodging. iOS: https://itunes.apple.com/us/app/base-directory/id423532315?mt=8
  Android:
  https://play.google.com/store/apps/details?id=and.dev.mil.trav&hl=en.

- MilSpaceA by Take-a-Hop is a great tool for Space-A travelers, with phone numbers for both recorded and live flight information. You can actually sign up for travel through the app. iOS and Android. http://www.takeahop.org/

- Ultimate U. S. Military Campgrounds for when we don't fly or if we want to stay put for a while.
  iOS: https://itunes.apple.com/us/app/the-ultimate-us-military-campground-project/id726475467?mt=8
  Android:
  https://play.google.com/store/apps/details?id=com.ultimatecampgrounds.mil&utm_source=downloadatoz.com.

You will also find numerous apps available for overseas travel. Consider these:

- Google Translate
  iOS: https://itunes.apple.com/us/app/google-translate/id414706506?mt=8
  Android:
  https://play.google.com/store/apps/details?id=com.google.android.apps.translate&hl=en

- iTranslate for language help. iOS and Android.
  http://www.itranslate.com/

- HyperDia for rail travel in Japan (this was priceless!)
  iOS: https://itunes.apple.com/us/app/hyperdia-by-voice/id379001449?mt=8
  Android:
  https://play.google.com/store/apps/details?id=com.hyperdia.android.activity&hl=en

- XE Currency for money conversion.
  http://www.xe.com/apps/

Find more to love at
http://www.timeout.com/travel/features/1169/the-worlds-50-best-travel-apps

IMPORTANT LINKS

U. S. STATE DEPARTMENT

- Online passport application
  https://travel.state.gov/content/passports/en/passports.html
  https://travel.state.gov/content/travel/en.html
- Travel advisories
  https://travel.state.gov/content/passports/en/alertswarnings.html

U. S. EMBASSY

https://www.usembassy.gov/

AIR MOBILITY COMMAND TRAVEL SITE

- PAX terminal Facebook links
  http://www.amc.af.mil/Home/AMC-Travel-Site/
- Baggage allowances
  http://www.amc.af.mil/Home/AMC-Travel-Site/Baggage-Allowances/
- Prohibited items
  http://www.amc.af.mil/Home/AMC-Travel-Site/Prohibited-Travel-Items/

Base information

http://www.militaryinstallations.dod.mil/MOS/f?p=MI:ENTRY:0.

USO locations

https://www.uso.org/locations

Space-A Message board

http://www.pepperd.com/

SpaceANet

http://spacea.net/

Mylar sleeping bag

https://beprepared.com/emergency-bag-reflective.html

DOCUMENTS TO READ/USE

International Security Advisory Board Report on Status of Forces Agreements – Information on SOFA

https://www.state.gov/documents/organization/236456.pdf

DOD Instruction 4515.13

http://execsec.defense.gov/Portals/34/Documents/Air%20Transportation%20Eligibility%20(DoDI%204515.13)%20January%202016.pdf

Patriot Express brochure

http://www.amc.af.mil/Portals/12/documents/2016%20PE%20Brochure.pdf?ver=2016-12-07-124504-557

In Person sign up form

http://www.amc.af.mil/Portals/12/documents/AFD-140926-014.pdf

Email sign up form

http://www.amc.af.mil/Portals/12/documents/AFD-150116-086.pdf

TIPS AND REMINDERS

Use common sense in EVERYTHING.

Follow the rules and don't assume anything. If you're not sure of correct procedures, ask questions. Make friends with the terminal agents at bases you want to fly to or from. They're your best research help. Every few days I scoured the Facebook pages of every terminal stateside to figure out which flights were available most often from that base. This helped me to plan the best route for our trip (even though it didn't go exactly as planned. But it did give me information for alternate routes in case of canceled or missed flights).

Expect delays. Be prepared to pay for lodging in case flights to/from your destination are not readily available, especially in cold climates. It's not hard to sleep on the beach, but how cold is the beach in Maryland during the winter? Although I budgeted $500 for our trip ($250 per week for two weeks), our actual expenses were much higher. I now plan for $100 per day for emergency funding for two.

Learn about your destinations, what services are available, and who to contact for information. Know in advance where to exchange currency. Most bases will have a bank/credit union.

Avoid over-packing. If you need an extra pair of shorts, a jacket, or a sweater, pick one up at the base thrift store or second-chance shop. Donate it back to the store when you leave. This is especially helpful if you end up in a colder region than you planned for. Plus, you'll have an ever-changing wardrobe!

Speaking of cold, remember that photo of Keith sitting outside the terminal at Joint Base Lewis-McChord? He doesn't look very warm, does he? Now I carry a couple of Mylar blankets along for insulating against the cold and for shade in the heat. They're inexpensive and very lightweight, so baggage weight is minimally affected. You can even buy a super lightweight emergency sleeping bag for under $5.

Be safe. Just like at home, always be aware of your surroundings.

Know where to get medical help if you need it. Have handy access to medicines, medical records, and emergency contacts. Ill health or accidents can never be predicted.

Check for updates! All of the information given here is current as of this writing (April, 2017). However, the world changes every day. While doing research for our own trip, I found several changes over a two-year period. It happens. Note the regs as you do your research, but be sure to check for updates before leaving home.

Check the State Department's Travel Advisories.

Check the Foreign Clearance Guide. If there are any restrictions or requirements for you to get into a country, you want to handle the details before you leave home. You may have to view the guide on the nearest base or check with your command for a copy of sections that apply to your trip.

Have patience. Most military personnel are young and do not have the life experience that you do. But they do know the rules. Work with them to accomplish your goals.

Relax. Things happen that could affect your attitude. Resolve to not let obstacles get under your skin. They are only problems to be solved. Enjoy the moment!

Made in the USA
Monee, IL
04 November 2026

67384431R00056